the BOOKS of MAGIC

Written by **Neil Gaiman**

Illustrated by John Bolton   Scott Hampton
Charles Vess   Paul Johnson

Lettered by Todd Klein

Cover Art by John Bolton

Karen Berger Editor – Original Series
Art Young Associate Editor – Original Series
Scott Nybakken Editor
Robbin Brosterman Design Director – Books
Louis Prandi Publication Design

Shelly Bond Executive Editor – Vertigo
Hank Kanalz Senior VP – Vertigo and Integrated Publishing

Diane Nelson President
Dan DiDio and Jim Lee Co-Publishers
Geoff Johns Chief Creative Officer
John Rood Executive VP – Sales, Marketing and Business Development
Amy Genkins Senior VP – Business and Legal Affairs
Nairi Gardiner Senior VP – Finance
Jeff Boison VP – Publishing Planning
Mark Chiarello VP – Art Direction and Design
John Cunningham VP – Marketing
Terri Cunningham VP – Editorial Administration
Alison Gill Senior VP – Manufacturing and Operations
Jay Kogan VP – Business and Legal Affairs, Publishing
Jack Mahan VP – Business Affairs, Talent
Nick Napolitano VP – Manufacturing Administration
Sue Pohja VP – Book Sales
Courtney Simmons Senior VP – Publicity
Bob Wayne Senior VP – Sales

Logo design by Richard Bruning/Brainstorm Unltd.

THE BOOKS OF MAGIC

Published by DC Comics.

DC Comics, 1700 Broadway, New York, NY 10019
A Warner Bros. Entertainment Company
Printed in the USA. First Printing.
ISBN: 978-1-4012-4686-0

Library of Congress Cataloging-in-Publication Data

Gaiman, Neil.
    The books of magic / Neil Gaiman, John Bolton, Charles Vess.
        p. cm.
    "Originally published in single magazine form in The Books of
Magic 1-4."
    ISBN 978-1-4012-4686-0 (alk. paper)
    1. Magic—Comic books, strips, etc. 2. Occultism—Comic books,
strips, etc. 3. Graphic novels. I. Bolton, John, 1951- II. Vess, Charles.
III. Title.
    PN6737.G3B63 2012
    741.5'942—dc23
                            2012033188

Table of Contents

INTRODUCTION

I once stopped in an odd little establishment in Ensenada, down in Baja, where a Hindu gentleman was selling tiny gold-plated orchids. He explained that they were real flowers, and that a process existed for plating them with that shiny metal without ruining their forms. Unable to resist, I said, "Sort of like gilding the lily, huh?" But his knowledge of the language had not progressed to the point of catching bad deadpan humor, and he responded, "No! No! Is not lily! Is orchid!"

Neil Gaiman does not really need an introduction. It would sort of be like — never mind.

He writes the award-winning SANDMAN series and is co-author with Terry Pratchett of the novel *Good Omens* which I have recommended to many and do yet again.

I first met Neil at an autographing session in Dallas. Most recently, I spent a pleasant evening with him and Steven Brust at the World Fantasy Convention in Phoenix, where we spoke of many things and I was reminded of something an older writer had told me long ago — namely, that editors only think that they're buying stories, that what they're really buying is the way a story is told. Look at Nick Bantock's fascinating *Griffin & Sabine*, where the medium is 95% of the enchantment.

Neil Gaiman is such a medium specialist. While his tales are gripping, moving, there is in particular the *way* of his stories to consider. I'm always fascinated by his point of attack and by the angles from which he views his people, settings, situations, actions. It's his approach that I study as much as the ideas he employs. And in the case of THE BOOKS OF MAGIC I am again fascinated. This time he has chosen for his subject the tale of initiation, the story of the magician's journey from innocence along the road to power.

The four volumes of THE BOOKS OF MAGIC, herein gathered, are a wonderful romp which I have read both backwards and forwards. In that they worked well for me in either direction, as well as in several odd shufflings of the deck, I feel free to talk about them in a variety of ways — none of which can really "give away the plot," because it's not that sort of story. While there is a storyline from which events depend, it is also a thematic tale, and I can talk about it at this level, choosing examples from wherever I would, without doing harm to anyone's reading pleasure.

Opening Joseph Campbell's *Hero with a Thousand Faces* to the Table of Contents and skipping over the Prologue wherein he will speak of the monomyth in general terms, we come to Part I, "The Adventure of the Hero," which is divided into four chapters: "Departure," "Initiation," "Return," and "The Keys." In that Campbell is examining the archetypes of all mythology here, and looking to describe a rhythm common to heroic fiction, I thought to hold it up next to THE BOOKS OF MAGIC to see how Neil's story compares with the hero's journey in world mythology at large.

Looking at the first volume as representing "The Departure," we see that it is indeed characterized by the five features Campbell discussed. The "Call to Adventure" comes simply enough in the midst of Timothy's mundane activity, skateboarding. The "Refusal of the Call" follows immediately, as Timothy flees the Stranger, Dr. Occult, and Mr. E — whereupon Constantine stops him, offering the classical "Supernatural Aid" by turning his yo-yo into an owl/familiar. "The Crossing of the First Threshold" then takes him on a journey back through time to beginnings. Then comes "The Belly of the Whale," the return to the center of things — the self-sacrificial experience, the learning of the price — which begins in the theater.

Looking on Book II as a continuation of "The Belly of the Whale," let us hold Book III up against the "Initiation" chapter. Campbell's breakdown here is "The Road of Trials," "The Meeting with the Goddess," "Woman as the Temptress," "Atonement with the Father," "Apotheosis," and "The Ultimate Boon."

All of these are encountered in Fairyland, with Titania as the goddess and the temptress, the father as the sleeping king under the mountain, and the apotheosis of sorts occurring on the receipt of the boon.

I won't even try to match things up for the final BOOK OF MAGIC. I will simply point out for homework that Campbell's next chapter, "The Return," contains the following sections: "Refusal of the Return," "The Magic Flight," "Rescue from Without," "The Crossing of the

Return Threshold," and "Freedom to Live."

This is one way to look at it. Sure, all of those things are there. It does not matter one whit, though, whether Neil cleverly synthesized the piece out of Campbell or whether he crafted a tale drawing upon similar sources so that such a thoroughgoing analysis must necessarily apply. Either way the result is a work worthy of respect.

One might remark on the sense of humor exhibited in Book III, where the hero and his companions are hanging around Baba Yaga's house, or the tangential nature of the future according to Book IV, or the blackness at the beginning of the universe, or at its end, view everything between as a cosmic day, and reduce all of the action to a solar myth; or, as I did earlier, one might play the sequence backwards, beginning with the playing-card archetypes and winding up regarding the Fall as an Ascension; or —

From a mundane standpoint, one might merely observe that Neil has arranged appearances here by every major occult figure in DC's history, to the possible end of introducing a new series character. And I do wonder whether Timothy will be back.

It is more than a clever story, however. It is rich and it is resonant. Like all good writing it causes the mind to wander off down byways by arousing speculations and leaving them to simmer. Why is Dr. Occult's female side so strong? What wonders will emerge from the mundane egg? What lock will Timothy's key one day fit? I like this allusiveness, this sense of depth. It entertains and engages me to see so much contained between these covers.

And Neil is fortunate here in having such interesting and talented colleagues as John Bolton, Scott Hampton, Charles Vess, and Paul Johnson rendering his visions into vivid images. And while people seldom comment on lettering because its job is generally to be unobtrusive, they also, for the same reason — habit — may not always note its subtle shifts in such places as the Museum of Ghosts sequences or Zatara's poem or the dialogue at Baba Yaga's or its alteration in various of the future sections — or simply not wonder why certain words get the bold face treatment. Todd Klein's sure hand is a definite part of the magic here.

Neil Gaiman is a writer I have resolved to watch, and so far the effort has never failed to return more than the price of admission to his worlds. Yes, I have enjoyed this story in many ways. It has been a journey worth taking. To say more would be to dip it in molten metal. Sweet dreams.

— Roger Zelazny
1993

Book I : The Invisible Labyrinth

"I DON'T WANT *ANYTHING* TO DO WITH IT."

"CONSTANTINE, I THOUGHT I HAD MADE MYSELF PERFECTLY CLEAR. WE HAVE NO *CHOICE.*"

"WHY *NOT?* AND DON'T LET'S START BLOODY DEBATING FREE WILL AGAIN, 'COS WE COULD BE HERE ALL WEEK."

"I THINK WHAT OUR FRIEND IS SAYING--"

I SAY THAT WE SHOULD *KILL* HIM. END THE MATTER THERE.

NOT *MY* FRIEND, MATE. NOT *THESE* DAYS.

--IF I MIGHT BE PERMITTED TO *FINISH,* MR. CONSTANTINE-- WHAT OUR FRIEND IS *TRYING* TO SAY IS SIMPLY *THIS:*

THE *BOY* IS A NATURAL FORCE, FOR *GOOD* OR FOR *EVIL,* FOR *MAGIC* OR FOR *SCIENCE,* AND IT IS UP TO *US* TO CHANNEL *THAT* FORCE FOR *GOOD.* AND, PERHAPS, FOR *MAGIC.*

AS RIGHTEOUS SOULS, IT IS OUR *RESPONSIBILITY* TO *TERMINATE* THE MATTER, TO ENSURE THIS POWER DOES NOT FALL INTO THE WRONG HANDS.

THERE WILL BE NO KILLING. OUR ROLE IS ONLY TO EDUCATE, TO OFFER HIM THE CHOICE.

"DOES ONE OFFER A *RABID DOG* A CHOICE?"

"HE IS A HUMAN CHILD. A NORMAL, HUMAN CHILD."

"THAT HAS NOTHING TO DO WITH IT, *E.* THE BOY IS NO DOG."

"NORMAL?"

ARE WE ALL IN AGREEMENT? *DOCTOR OCCULT?*

I AGREE. I WILL SHOW HIM THE FAR LANDS.

"MISTER E?"

IF YOU ARE TOO *SOFT* TO DISPOSE OF HIM, THEN I SUPPOSE YOU MUST *EDUCATE* HIM. IF HE *GETS* THAT FAR THEN I WILL TAKE HIM TO THE *END.*

"CONSTANTINE?"

YEAH, FAIR ENOUGH. I'LL GIVE HIM THE GRAND TOUR, INTRODUCE HIM TO THE RUNNERS, GIVE HIM AN IDEA OF THE STARTING PRICE.

EVERYWHERE. IT'S COMING FROM EVERYWHERE.

BOY! DO YOU BELIEVE IN MAGIC?

HUH?

WHO THE HELL WAS THAT? A WEIRDO? A PERVERT? I NEARLY JUMPED OUT OF MY SKIN.

STILL, LOST HIM NOW.

YEAH? SO WHAT *ARE YOU* CALLED?

MEN CALL ME DR. OCCULT.

AND *I* AM KNOWN AS *MISTER E.*

MYSTERY?

MISTER E.

DID YOU MAKE THAT UP YOURSELF?

SO WHO ARE *YOU*?

LET ME GUESS... um... "MISTER WEARS A BLACK COAT"? "PROFESSOR ESOTERIC"? "CAPTAIN NOBODY"?

I CLAIM NEITHER A NAME NOR A TITLE, TIMOTHY HUNTER, ALTHOUGH I HOPE ONE DAY, PERHAPS, YOU WILL CALL ME FRIEND. UNTIL THAT TIME I MUST REMAIN A STRANGER.

I DON'T BELIEVE ANY OF THIS! WHAT'S GOING ON? SOME KIND OF *JOKE*? CANDID CAMERA?

NO JOKES. NO TRICKS.

WE'RE HERE TO GIVE YOU A CHOICE. DO YOU WANT MAGIC IN YOUR LIFE, CHILD?

THIS IS *STUPID.* FOUR LOONIES...THERE'S NO SUCH *THING* AS MAGIC.

MAGIC.

COULD I... COULD I DO THAT?

IF THAT IS THE ROUTE YOU WISH TO WALK, TIMOTHY. THAT IS WHY WE ARE HERE.

OUR ROLE IS TO EDUCATE, TIMOTHY. TO SHOW YOU THE PATH OF ENCHANTMENT, OF THE ART, OF GRAMARYE AND GLAMOUR-- WHETHER YOU CHOOSE TO WALK IT AFTER THAT WILL BE YOUR OWN AFFAIR.

WILL YOU COME WITH ME, TIMOTHY HUNTER?

IF I COULD DO THAT STUFF THEY'D HAVE TO TREAT ME DIFFERENT. THAT'S FOR CERTAIN.

I WOULDN'T HAVE TO TAKE ANY CRAP FROM ANYBODY. NOT EVER.

NOT EVER AGAIN.

I'LL COME WITH YOU. WHERE ARE WE GOING?

THROUGH THE DOOR.

DO YOU GET PAID FOR SPEAKING IN RIDDLES OR SOMETHING?

THE PAST IS ALWAYS KNOCKING AT THE DOOR, TRY-ING TO BREAK THROUGH, INTO TODAY.

WE WILL SEE THE PAST, BUT WE CANNOT INFLUENCE IT.

WALK WITH ME, THROUGH THE DOOR.

IT IS A CRY OF PAIN, CHILD; THE PAIN THAT COMES WITH BIRTH.

BIRTH?

IT'S SO LOUD.

AND IT HURTS...

OWW...

YOUR PAIN IS ONLY THE TINIEST FRACTION OF THE PAIN THAT BROUGHT FORTH, FROM THE VOID...

LIGHT.

TIME.

HEAT.

LIFE.

"THEY LOOK LIKE...
ANGELS."

"INDEED."

"WHO'S HE?"

"THE PROUDEST OF THEM
ALL, AND THE MOST
BEAUTIFUL."

"WHAT'S HIS NAME?"

"...OH. BLOODY HELL."

"LUCIFER. THE LIGHTBRINGER

WALKING THE
MAZE, AGAIN.

FOLLOW ME; INTO THE CAVES,
WALKING NARROW, WINDING
PATHS, LOSING OURSELVES
IN THE PAST. LOSING EVERYTHING.

THE RED FLAME FLICKERS ON THE WALL OF THE CAVE
[SMEARED WITH OCHRES, BERRY DYE, CHARCOAL]
MAKING THE GREAT ELK MOVE,
MAKING THE MASTODON BREATHE,
MAKING THE HUNTERS RACE AND KILL.

WATCH THEM SEEKING TO PLACATE
    AND UNDERSTAND THE WORLD ABOVE.
THIS THEY KNOW:
THIS THEY UNDERSTAND:
THERE IS DARKNESS, EVERYWHERE, OUTSIDE.

THE DARK IS EVERYWHERE; AND THOUGH THE SUN COMES UP,
AND THOUGH THE FIRES BLOSSOM, AND ARE TAMED,
THE DARKNESS IS THERE.
THE DARKNESS IS WAITING.

AND THE THINGS IN THE DARKNESS
THAT WHISPER BEFORE THEY FEAST,
THEY ARE TO BE PLACATED AND PERSUADED,
THEY ARE TO BE LOVED AND SACRIFICED TO,
THEY ARE TO BE PRAYED TO AND DISTRUSTED.

AND SO THERE IS MAGIC.

35

THE RISE OF EMPIRES;
MAYFLY NAMES THAT
FLICKER AND ARE GONE.

FROM FAR CH'IN AND DISTANT CHU, BY THE WATERS OF THE
    YELLOW RIVER
THE DRAGONS ARE WALKING, DISCOURSING IN SAGE ANALECTS,
"REVERE SPIRITS, BUT KEEP THEM AT A DISTANCE",
THE LORDS OF THE NINE HEAVENS RIDE CHARIOTS OF ORCHIDS,
AND THE WU WOMAN DREAMS OF DARK BAMBOO GROVES,
THE LORD OF THE EAST COMES TO LOOSEN HER ROBES OF WHITE RAINBO
SHE DREAMS THEY RIDE IN A FISH-SCALE CHARIOT,
FLANKED BY GRIFFINS,
AND IN THE SKY PAPER KITES ARE FLUTTERING.

WHEN SHE WAKES HE IS GONE,
    FOR A WHILE SHE LOITERS, PACING TO AND FRO.

SHE DREAMS AGAIN:
FROM MEETINGS AND PARTINGS NONE CAN EVER ESCAPE;

NOR FROM MAGIC.

麻鬼
法

IN the nile delta the sands whisper
of dog-faced gods,
azure scarab beetles,
tall shadow women
that pad like great lions across the dunes,
blood and honey dripping from their jaws.
And magic.

IN THE LANDS OF OLIVE AND LAUREL,
WHERE THE GODS WALK,
WE WATCH A SOLDIER PISS AROUND HIS CLOTHES,
LOPE AWAY A WOLF.

—— AT THE HEART OF EVERY MYSTERY,
WHISPERS THE TWICE-BORN BOY, WHO ROSE FROM THE DEAD,
—— IS THE GRAIN OF MY CORN, AND THE WINE OF MY BLOOD.
DRAMA, VINES AND GOAT-FEET FOLLOW HIM INTO THE WORLD.

THE WITCH-QUEEN ALWAYS HAS THREE FACES; WHO WAITS AT THE CROSSROADS,
    FOR YOUR SACRIFICE;
WAITS IN THE UNDERWORLD,
IN THE SACRED GROVES,   ABRACADABRA.
IN THE MOON.   ABRAXAS...
SHE SITS BENEATH A DEAD KING, HANGING FROM A TREE BRANCH,
AND WILL SHOW YOU ALL MANNER OF ELEGANT CHARMS.   MAGIC.

THE DIFFERENCE IN VIEWPOINT.

SCIENCE IS A WAY OF TALKING ABOUT THE UNIVERSE IN WORDS THAT BIND IT TO A COMMON REALITY.

MAGIC IS A METHOD OF TALKING TO THE UNIVERSE IN WORDS THAT IT CANNOT IGNORE.

THE TWO ARE RARELY COMPATIBLE.

SO WHAT ARE YOU SAYING? THAT MAGIC DIED OUT BY MY TIME?

NO. BUT WILD MAGIC IS A THING OF THE PAST.

AND, SINCE THERE ARE ALWAYS THOSE WHO WOULD BURN THOSE THEY PERCEIVE AS WITCHES, MANY TRUE MAGICIANS ADOPTED NEW GARB, AVOIDING RECOGNITION BY DISGUISING THEIR PLUMAGE.

I WILL SHOW YOU SOME OF THEM.

COME. LET US WALK FURTHER.

THE EARLY DECADES OF YOUR OWN CENTURY.

A TOWER IN SALEM; THE ROOM WITH NO DOORS.

HIS NAME IS KENT NELSON. HE IS ALSO CALLED FATE. DR. FATE.

THE HELM IS CALLED NABU. HE FOUND IT IN A PYRAMID. HE IS A MAGICIAN, AND HE CONSIDERS HIMSELF A HERO.

AT NIGHT THE HELMET MURMURS TO HIM. WHISPERS THE PAST, WHISPERS A WORLD OF PURE ORDER, DEAD AND STILL.

AS TIME GOES ON, THE MASK BECOMES THE FACE. IT'S DESTINY, PERHAPS.

OR FATE.

TALKING BACKWARDS
BECAUSE TIME WILL NOT GO BACKWARDS
BECAUSE I WILL WALK UNTIL I SEE AN ANSWER
GRAFFITI WRITTEN BACKWARDS ON THE WALL INVISIBLE
BECAUSE I AM GETTING AHEAD...
WATCH MY DUST.

THE FEAR IS OF THE UNKNOWN.
WE KILL THE THINGS WE DO NOT UNDERSTAND.
HERE:
　　TALK BACKWARDS
　　ANIMATE A DREAM
HERE:
　　TALK BACKWARDS
　　GLAMOURS MASK THE FEAR.

THE NEED TO GET AHEAD, THE BURNING NEED.
(WATCH MY DUST, MY DAUGHTER,
　　WATCH MY DUST.)
I NEED MORE THAN ILLUSION,
WE DO IT WITH MIRRORS,
AND RABBITS
ATHANORS
AND DOVES...

WHEN THE MAGIC APPEARS, WHEN THE LIGHTS GO UP,
WHEN I'M DRESSED IN MY TOP HAT
AND MY COAT OF MANY POCKETS
WHEN I'M TALKING BACKWARDS...

THEN I KNEW THAT I WAS EDGING THROUGH THE MAZE.
AND ONCE I HAD GONE PAST DELUSION
PAST THE OTHERS
ALL "THE GREAT," "THE AMAZING," "THE MASTER OF ILLUSION,"
PAST ALL OF THEM
ONCE THEY HAD SEEN MY DUST,
I FOUND

　　EMPTINESS
　　THE HOLLOW PLACE AT THE CENTER OF
　　　THE MAZE
　　NO RETURNING
　　NO WAY BACK

　　NOT EVEN SPEAKING BACKWARDS
　　NOT EVEN WALKING BACKWARDS

I THOUGHT I HAD FOUND MY WAY TO
　THE CENTER OF THE INVISIBLE LABYRINTH;
AND I HAD—PERHAPS—DISCOVERED
NO MORE THAN THE ENTRANCE.

WATCH MY DUST.

I RETREATED INTO SAFETY,
THE WORLD OF ILLUSION,
IN THE STAGE,
IN THE FOOTLIGHTS,
ALL EYES UPON ME AND NO ONE REALLY SEEING,

BECAUSE I DO NOT TALK BACKWARDS:
BECAUSE I DO NOT SAY,

(THGIN EMOCEB SEILFRETTUB)
AND THE NIGHT DOES NOT BECOME BUTTERFLIES.
I GIVE NOTHING OF MYSELF TO THE AUDIENCE,
AS I DO IT WITH MIRRORS
AND STRING
AND SLEIGHT
　　THE DELUSION OF ILLUSION AND THE HAND
　　　DECEIVES THE EYE...

MY LIFE IS STROBED LIKE LIGHTNING BY A FOLLOW-
　SPOT,
AND LOOKING BACKWARDS I CAN ONLY SEE
THE CORPSES OF THE ANIMALS AND BIRDS
WHO STRUTTED WITH ME ON THE DARKENED STAGE
AND HELPED ME FOOL THEM ALL.

CHARMS OF BIRDS
　　AND HATSFUL OF DEAD RABBITS.

I TAKE MY LAST BOW WITH PRIDE, AS PROUDLY AS
　BEFITS A CONJURE MAN
GOING DOWN IN FLAMES,
UP AS SMOKE.

THERE IS NO WALKING BACKWARDS,
AND I AM LOST IN THE LABYRINTH INVISIBLE.
I CANNOT RETRACE MY STEPS.

I WROTE MY NAME ON THE WALL OF THE
INVISIBLE LABYRINTH.
I WAS SO DILIGENT IN MY STUDIES;
GAVE MY WHOLE TIME AND HEART TO THE
PURSUIT.

I WROTE MY NAME, BUT I CAN FIND IT
NO LONGER;
MY ASHES BLOW LIKE DUST AROUND THE
INVISIBLE LABYRINTH.

I-HAVE-SEEN-GOOD-AND-I-HAVE-SEEN-EVIL. AND-NOW I-AM-DEAD. I-HAVE-BEEN-GOOD-AND-I-HAVE-BEEN-EVIL.

AND-NOW-I-AM-DEAD. LOOK-O-N...M-Y...W-O-R-K-S...

WHO'S THAT?

NOTHING'S FREE.

WOULD YOU LIKE IT?

I DON'T KNOW.

A SENSIBLE ATTITUDE.

YOU HAVE BEGUN TO WALK A PATH INTO KNOWLEDGE, CHILD.

BY THE END OF YOUR PATH YOU WILL HAVE THE INFORMATION TO DECIDE WHAT IT IS YOU DO WANT.

WHERE ARE WE?

IT'S AN AEROPLANE. BIG METAL THING, FLIES THROUGH THE AIR, SENDS YOUR LUGGAGE TO HONG KONG.

ONLY *WE* HAVEN'T *GOT* ANY LUGGAGE, SO THAT'S ALL RIGHT.

UM. HOW DID WE *GET* HERE? LAST THING I REMEMBER, WE WERE IN THE SHOPPING PRECINCT, AND *YOU* WERE SAYING...

I SAID I'D BE *INTRODUCING* YOU TO A FEW PEOPLE, DIDN'T I? WELL, *MOST* OF THEM LIVE IN AMERICA, SO THAT'S WHERE WE'RE GOING.

BUT I DON'T *REMEMBER* ANYTHING-- AND I DON'T HAVE A *PASSPORT*.

ME NEITHER. I HAD ONE ONCE, BUT I *LOST* IT. KEEP MEANING TO GET A NEW ONE, BUT I NEVER GET AROUND TO IT.

BUT HOW DID WE GET ONTO THE *PLANE?* AND WHAT HAPPENS WHEN WE WANT TO GET *OFF?*

YOU *WORRY* TOO MUCH, YOU KNOW THAT?

NOW, YOU SLEPT THROUGH A ROTTEN MOVIE, AND YOU MISSED A CHOICE BETWEEN *TWO* INEDIBLES FOR LUNCH.

WE LAND IN NEW YORK IN HALF AN HOUR, AND I'M GOING UP FRONT TO CHAT TO A RATHER NICE LADY FLIGHT ATTENDANT.

OH. RIGHT.

HELLO. YOU'RE TIM HUNTER, *AREN'T* YOU?

YES.

BRAND. BOSTON BRAND. PLEASED TO MEETCHA. THERE'S BEEN A *LOT* OF NOISE ABOUT *YOU* IN THE NETHERWORLDS, KIDDO.

HAS THERE?

SURE. I WAS *JUST* TALKIN' TO A DUDE WHO GOT HIMSELF *KILLED* TRYING TO FIND OUT WHERE YOU WERE.

LOOK, I HATE TO BE PERSONAL, BUT... ARE YOU *MAD*?

NOT THAT I'M AWARE OF.

IT'S JUST I FIGURED IT WAS *YOU* OR *ME*, AND THAT MEANS IT'S PROBABLY *ME*.

YEAH? SO THIS GUY WAS PART OF THE COLD FLAME, OR THE BLOOD RED MOON, OR THE DARK CIRCLE -- *ONE* OF THOSE SPOOKSHOWS.

THEY'RE TRYING TO *FIND* YOU, KIDDO. YOU GOTTA TAKE *CARE* OF YOURSELF.

I *DON'T* KNOW WHAT YOU'RE TALKING ABOUT, AND TO BE HONEST, I DON'T *CARE*.

FAMOUS LAST WORDS, KIDDO.

MINE WERE: "GEE, FROM UP HERE IT ALMOST LOOKS LIKE THAT GUY WITH THE *HOOK'S* HOLDING A *RIFLE...*"

ANYTHING INTERESTING HAPPEN WHEN I WAS GONE, THEN?

NOPE.

FAIR ENOUGH.

59

ENTER, FREELY AND UNAFRAID...

JOHN CONSTANTINE! HOW *DARE* YOU COME INTO THIS PLACE. *GET OUT!*

UM. MADAME X. LOOKING LOVELY AS USUAL. YOU HAVEN'T AGED A DAY.

DO *NOT* ATTEMPT TO *FLATTER* ME, YOU, YOU *SNEAK-THIEF!* IF YOU THINK I'VE *FORGOTTEN* HOW YOU TREATED ME THE *LAST* TIME YOU WERE HERE...

...HOW YOU *WORMED* YOUR WAY INTO MY CONFIDENCE, PURELY IN ORDER TO *STEAL* THE *WIND'S EGG.*

I SHOULD *REND YOU LIMB FROM LIMB.* I SHOULD SET *HARPIES* TO TEAR OUT YOUR *EYES* AND FOUL YOUR *FOOD.*

HOW YOU *DARE* TO STEP INTO MY HOME, INTO MY *PLACE OF POWER.* WHY, I'VE A GOOD MIND TO...

UM. WOULD IT HELP IF I SAID I WAS *SORRY?*

I WILL GIVE YOU JUST *TEN* SECONDS TO GET OUT OF HERE, JOHN CONSTANTINE. *THEN* I WILL, *I WILL...*

TIM, GO AND STAND OUTSIDE A SEC, WILL YOU?

60

NO PROBLEM. I CAN TAKE CARE OF HIM.

YEAH. I'M SURE IT'S THE BOY.

COME ON IN, TIM. LET ME INTRODUCE YOU PROPERLY.

TIM, THIS LADY'S CALLED MADAME XANADU. MADAME X, THIS IS TIM HUNTER.

I AM PLEASED TO MEET YOU, CHILD. THE CONSTANTINE HAS TOLD ME A LITTLE ABOUT YOU. SIT DOWN.

I WILL READ YOUR CARDS.

WE'RE IN A HURRY, MADAME X. CAN'T WE SKIP IT?

NO. BUT WE WILL DO THE SIMPLEST OF READINGS.

SHUFFLE THE PACK, UNTIL YOU FEEL COMFORTABLE WITH IT, THEN HAND IT BACK TO ME.

FOUR CARDS: EVERYTHING IS HERE, CHILD. ELEMENTS, HUMORS, AND THE CORNERS OF THE WORLD. HMM. ALL MAJOR ARCANA, ALTHOUGH I'D'VE BEEN SURPRISED HAD THEY BEEN ANYTHING ELSE. SO...

"THE *FIRST* CARD TELLS US WHERE YOU HAVE *COME* FROM.

"THE *ANCIENT*. ONE WHO OBSERVES, BUT REMAINS SILENT. A WISE MAN WILL-- NO, *HAS* ALREADY-- INTRODUCED YOU TO SECRET KNOWLEDGE. SOMEONE TERRIBLY *OLD*, WHO DOES *NOT* SOCIALIZE. I SEE TIMES GONE.

THE HERMIT.

"THE *SECOND* CARD TELLS US WHERE YOU ARE RIGHT *NOW*.

"THE *WHEEL OF FORTUNE*. SOMEONE UNRELIABLE, A *GAMBLER*. SEIZE YOUR OPPORTUNITIES, WHEN THEY ARE PRESENTED TO YOU. *ADVENTURE* COMES TO YOU, AND *DANGER*-- YOU ARE IN *GREAT DANGER*, IF I AM NOT MISTAKEN. AND I'M *NOT*.

WHEEL of FORTUNE.

"THE *THIRD* CARD TELLS US WHERE YOU ARE *GOING*...

"THE *EMPRESS*. STRANGE. SOMEONE WHO UNDERSTANDS-- OR IS IN TOUCH WITH-- THEIR FEMALE SIDE. A WOMAN-- POSSIBLY MORE THAN ONE WOMAN LOOMS LARGE. SHE GUARDS SOMETHING WHICH SHE MAY YET GIVE TO YOU. A DAY WORLD, AND A NIGHT WORLD...

THE EMPRESS.

"AND THE *LAST* CARD TELLS US WHERE IT WILL ALL *TAKE* YOU.

"*JUSTICE*, REVERSED. HMM-- SOMEONE CLOSE TO YOU AGAIN A DECISION TO BE MADE. THE *BLIND JUDGE* PREPARED TO CUT THE *BABY* IN HALF. A TIME OF GREAT *DARKNESS*."

JUSTICE.

HMMM... THESE CARDS MIGHT BE *PEOPLE,* OR *CONDITIONS,* OR *TIMES.* OR MORE...

FOUR *MEN?* OR THREE MEN AND ONE WOMAN...

I AM *SORRY.* WITH MORE TIME, PERHAPS... BUT YOU MUST BE OFF, I SEE. YOU *RIDE* THE *WHEEL OF FORTUNE,* TRAVEL WITH THE *GAMBLER.*

GOOD LUCK, BOY.

BEWARE JUSTICE.

NORMALLY I EXPECT A *GIFT* FROM MY QUERENTS. BUT I THINK IN *THIS* CASE, I HAVE SOMETHING FOR *YOU.*

HERE, TIMOTHY. BEFORE YOU GO

YO-YO! IT *IS* YO-YO, ISN'T IT!

IS *CORRIGAN* ABOUT YET?

I WOULD EXPECT SO.

AND HIS OTHER HALF?

HE GOES WHERE CORRIGAN DOES, *THESE DAYS.*

RIGHT, WE'LL HEAD ON UPSTAIRS, THEN. TAKE *CARE,* LOVE.

WHAT DID YOU RECKON TO THE READING?

I DON'T KNOW. SHE DIDN'T SEEM THAT PLEASED TO SEE YOU. WERE YOU *CLOSE?*

MM. *ONCE.* THERE'S A *LOT* A YOUNG LAD CAN LEARN FROM AN *OLDER WOMAN.*

AND DID YOU REALLY STEAL HER, WHAT WAS IT, *WIND EGG?*

IN A MANNER OF SPEAKING. I *MEANT* TO RETURN IT, BUT IT GOT SLIGHTLY *BROKEN* IN A SCUFFLE WITH A *TROLL.* IN *BIRMINGHAM.*

"OH, *SURE. THERE* ARE TROLLS IN *BIRMINGHAM* ALL RIGHT."

"IF YOU KNOW WHERE TO LOOK, YES."

IS HE *GAY?* THIS JIM CORACLE BLOKE.

CORRIGAN. NOT THAT I KNOW OF. *WHY?*

CORRIGAN DETECTIVE AGENCY

WELL, YOU WERE TALKING ABOUT HIS OTHER HALF, AND *SHE* SAID *HE,* AND...

HELLO. DO YOU HAVE AN APPOINTMENT?

NOT AS SUCH. CAN YOU TELL YOUR BOSS THAT MISTER CONSTANTINE IS HERE TO SEE HIM?

YOU SEE, CORRIGAN IS DEAD.

DEAD?

SORT OF. HE'S BEEN *DEAD* SINCE THE LATE 1930s, AS I UNDER-STAND IT. ONLY HE GOT BROUGHT *BACK.*

AND SOMETHING *ELSE* GOT BROUGHT BACK *WITH* HIM--THERE'S DIFFERENCES OF OPINION ABOUT EXACTLY *WHAT.*

"I MEAN, THERE'S A SCHOOL OF THOUGHT THAT SAYS IT'S HIS *SOUL,* SUPERCHARGED, AS IT WERE. AND THERE'S *ANOTHER* SCHOOL OF THOUGHT THAT SUGGESTS IT'S SOMETHING FAR *OLDER.*"

WHATEVER IT IS, *SOMETIMES* IT'S PRACTICALLY THE MOST *POWERFUL* THING IN THE *UNIVERSE*. SOMETIMES IT'S LITTLE MORE THAN A BLOKE IN *WHITE TIGHTS* AND A *GREEN HOOD*.

IT'S BEEN UP AND DOWN THE OCCULT LEAGUE TABLES FASTER THAN A WHORE'S DRAWERS.

IT'S CALLED--

IT'S CALLED THE *SPECTRE*. *WHO* ARE YOU? *HOW* DO YOU KNOW ALL THIS? COME ON INSIDE.

I GET AROUND, BOSS. YOU KNOW HOW IT IS. JOHN CONSTANTINE. ASK YOUR OTHER HALF-- *HE* KNOWS ME.

CORRIGAN, TIM HUNTER. TIMOTHY, THIS IS THE *LATE* JIM CORRIGAN.

UM, HULLO. I'VE NEVER MET A DEAD PERSON BEFORE.

SO, YOU'RE ENGLISH, HUH? SYE, MITE, 'OWS ABOWT A STYKE AN KIDNEY POI, 'EN A POINT OF YER BIST IYLE?

SORRY?

TALK *JUST* LIKE A COCKNEY, DON'T I? Y'SEE, I WENT TO ENGLAND A COUPLA TIMES WHEN I WAS WITH *NYPD*. YOU OUGHT TO ARM YOUR COPPERS. HEH-- BUT *YOU* CALL THEM *BOBBIES*, RIGHT?

NOT ME. I THINK YOU'RE THINKING OF SOMEONE ELSE.

YOU GUYS ON *VACATION?*

NOT REALLY. MISTER CONSTANTINE IS TEACHING ME A BIT ABOUT MAGIC. INTRODUCING ME TO PEOPLE.

"*GREAT* TO MEET YOU. IF EVER YOU NEED A PRIVATE DETECTIVE, BE SURE TO CALL THE CORRIGAN AGENCY. *RIGHT?*"

"UH--IS THAT AN *OWL?*"

NO, IT'S MY YO-YO.

I *LOVE* YOUR BRITISH SENSE OF HUMOR. BENNY HILL AND THAT *MONTY PYTHON* GUY...

YOU ARE TIMOTHY HUNTER. YOU ARE JOHN CONSTANTINE.

WHAT WAS *THAT* ABOUT?

SOMEONE TRIED TO KILL YOU.

OH.

THE FORCES OF DARKNESS ARE ALWAYS AMONG US, CHILD. AND THE LIGHT CRIES OUT EVER FOR VENGEANCE.

THERE IS LIGHT AND THERE IS DARKNESS; AND I CANNOT REST UNTIL THE DARKNESS IS DESTROYED AND THE LIGHT SHINES INTO THE HEARTS OF ALL.

OH.

I FELL FROM GRACE. NOW I AM CONDEMNED TO WALK THE SHADOW WORLD. ONCE, IT WAS I WHO CAST THE SHADOW...

THEY WILL TRY TO KILL YOU, AND THEY WILL TRY TO SEDUCE YOU. STAY PURE, CHILD. STAY PURE.

UM. THANKS.

RIGHT--I THINK I'VE GOT WHAT WE CAME FOR. *CHEERS.*

PIP-PIP, OWLD CHEPS!

BERK.

UM... JOHN? WASN'T HE OUR TAXI DRIVER?

WAS BEING THE OPERATIVE WORD. YEAH.

CHRIST--I FIGURED WE'D HAVE A GOOD *WEEK* BEFORE THEY GOT ON TO US.

BUGGER.

68

TIMOTHY HUNTER. JOHN CONSTANTINE. I HAVE A MESSAGE FOR YOU BOTH.

TIM, THIS IS ONE OF THE GOOD GUYS.

MISTER FATE. YEAH, I SAW HIM IN THE PAST. HE USED TO BE KENT NELSON.

DOCTOR FATE. TRUE, WE USED TO BE KENT NELSON, CHILD. AND HE IS PART OF US NOW.

FUNNY-- I WAS PLANNING ON INCLUDING YOU IN TIM'S MAGICAL MYSTERY TOUR. ONLY I SUSPECT THE TOUR MAY HAVE TO BE CALLED OFF.

I BRING WORD, FROM YOUR THREE COMRADES-IN-ARMS.

THEY'RE REALLY JUST ACQUAINTANCES-IN-BIG-COATS.

THE FORCES OF DARKNESS HAVE PUT A PRICE ON THE CHILD'S HEAD.

CONSTANTINE-- YOU MUST FIND SANCTUARY FOR HIM, THEN ASSIST YOUR BROTHERS IN THEIR BATTLE AGAINST THE POWERS OF NIGHT.

IS THIS A SPECIFIC AND LOCALIZED BATTLE, OR JUST A SORT OF VAGUELY GENERAL ONGOING THING?

FIRST FIND SANCTUARY FOR TIMOTHY, JOHN CONSTANTINE.

I HATE THIS BUSINESS. IF I DIDN'T HATE GETTING UP IN THE MORNINGS MORE, I'D CHUCK IT ALL IN AND GET A PROPER JOB TOMORROW.

YOU WILL LEAVE HERE IMMEDIATELY.

18 ENGINE CO. 18

ALL THINGS ARE DIVIDED INTO THE TWIN FORCES OF *ORDER* AND *CHAOS,* FOREVER CONTENDING FOR DOMINANCE.

LIFE IS SOMETHING THAT OCCURS IN THE *INTERFACE*; *NOT* IN THE WRITHING DISCORD OF UTTER CHAOS, *NOR* IN THE FLATLINE PERFECTION OF PURE ORDER, BUT SOMEWHERE BETWEEN.

CHAOS VERSUS ORDER INDEED. I THOUGHT *EVERYONE* HAD HEARD OF *FRACTALS* THESE DAYS.

THERE'S *NO* CHAOS, *NO* ORDER; JUST *PATTERNS* OF DIFFERENT LEVELS OF COMPLEXITY.

WOULD YOU LIKE ANYTHING TO *DRINK*, SIR?

GIN AND TONIC, PLEASE, LOVE. *TIM?*

CAN I HAVE A *SOUTHERN* COMFORT?

HE'LL HAVE A GINGER ALE.

BUT--

LOOK, THE *LAST* THING I NEED ON MY HANDS IS A DRUNK TWELVE-YEAR-OLD.

I'M OFF TO THE LOO. DON'T GO ANYWHERE.

PSST-- *KIDDO.*

YEAH?

IT'S *ME.* BOSTON BRAND.

HUH?

YOU REMEMBER-- I WAS SITTING *NEXT* TO YOU ON THE PLANE COMING INTO *JFK.*

YOU'VE LOST WEIGHT. AND CHANGED COLOR.

YEAH. WELL, THAT'S BECAUSE THIS ISN'T MY *BODY.* I'M JUST, Y'KNOW, *BORROWING* IT, TO *TALK* TO YOU. YOU SEE, I'M *DEAD.*

WHAT'S SO FUNNY?

WELL, EARLIER TODAY I WAS SAYING THAT I'D NEVER *MET* A DEAD PERSON BEFORE, AND NOW I'VE MET *TWO* IN A DAY.

THREE, IF YOU COUNT THE TAXI DRIVER, ONLY *HE STOPPED TALKING* WHEN HE DIED.

THEY SAY THE THIRD TIME'S THE CHARM.

SO WHAT DO YOU MAKE OF *CONSTANTINE?*

HE'S ALL RIGHT, I SPOSE -- EASIER TO TALK TO THAN THE OTHER THREE. ONLY THING I CAN'T FIGURE OUT IS HOW WE GET FROM *PLACE TO PLACE...*

THAT ONE'S EASY, KIDDO. HE'S RIDING THE *SYNCHRONICITY FREEWAY,* AND SO EVERYTHING JUST FALLS INTO PLACE; *TIME, MOVEMENT,* EVEN *DISTANCE* JUST SIT UP AND BEG FOR HIM.

YOU'RE HAVING AN *ADVENTURE,* KIDDO. IF YOU SURVIVE IT, IT'LL BE *FUN.*

I'LL DO WHAT *I* CAN.

ANYWAY, I'VE BEEN TRYING TO TELL YOU SOMETHING *IMPORTANT.* LISTEN --

MORNING STAR

BOY NUMBER 8'S BODY FOUND IN SEWER

WHO'S YOUR FRIEND?

UM, THIS IS BOSTON BRAND.

BRAND? NAH. MY NAME'S *MATTHESON.* WHOA -- I FEEL SORTA *DIZZY...*

THAT IS OUR OBJECTIVE, MY FRIENDS. THE *CITADEL* OF THE *COLD FLAME.*

DARK WALKER, THERE ARE ONLY *THREE* OF US. DO YOU *SERIOUSLY* THINK WE CAN STOP THEM?

RIGHT IS ON *OUR* SIDE. OF *COURSE* WE CAN.

RIGHT IS, ALAS, *NO* GUARANTEE OF SUCCESS, E. BUT WE HAVE TO TRY.

IF WE CANNOT DESTROY THE HEAD, THEN THE ARMS WILL REACH OUT AND KILL TIMOTHY HUNTER; AND I CANNOT PERMIT THAT.

WE SHOULD *LET* THEM *KILL* HIM. IT WOULD ELIMINATE ALL POTENTIAL PROBLEMS.

NO.

MY *FATHER* USED TO SAY, *BACON* IS NOT THE *ONLY* THING THAT'S *CURED* BY *HANGING* FROM A *TREE.*

AND WE KNOW TOO WELL WHAT HAPPENED TO YOUR FATHER, E.

LIES! FOUL, WICKED, BLASPHEMOUS *LIES!* MY FATHER WAS A *GREAT* MAN, BROUGHT LOW BY SMALL-MINDED *FOOLS.*

ENOUGH BICKERING. IF YOU ARE NOT WITH US, E, YOU ARE FREE TO LEAVE.

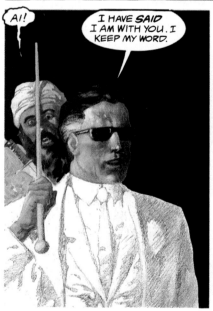

AI!

I HAVE *SAID* I AM WITH YOU. I KEEP MY WORD.

GOOD. IT WILL BE *DAWN* SOON. WE MUST FORMULATE A PLAN OF ATTACK. *TOMORROW* IS ALL HALLOW'S EVE, AFTER ALL.

AND WE MUST PRAY THAT *CONSTANTINE* KNOWS WHAT HE IS DOING.

OH.

OH DEAR.

CHRIST!

YOU GOTTA TAKE BETTER CARE OF THE KIDDO THAN THAT, CONSTANTINE.

MUUURP.

WHAT WAS THAT ABOUT?

HAVEN'T THE FOGGIEST.

LET'S GET MOVING. WE'VE GOT TO GET YOU SOMEWHERE SAFE.

WINTER'S HOUSE'LL BE THE BEST PLACE FOR US. IT'S JUST ROUND HERE.

BARON WINTER'S AN OLD BUDDY OF MINE. WON'T *HE* BE PLEASED TO SEE US...

Ding Dong

'ULLO, BARON.

OH. IT'S *YOU*.

LIKE A BAD PENNY. PLEASED TO SEE US?

CONSTANTINE, I AM *ENTERTAINING*. I HAVE A DINNER GUEST HERE. *PLEASE LEAVE*.

DINNER? BRILLIANT. WE'RE BOTH *STARVING*. THIS IS TIMOTHY HUNTER. HE'S GOING TO BE A TOP CLASS MAGICIAN ONE DAY, IF HE *WANTS* TO BE. TROUBLE IS THAT *SOME* PEOPLE ARE TRYING TO *KILL* HIM.

SO WE'VE COME TO *YOU* FOR SANCTUARY.

GO *AWAY*. GOODBYE. LOVELY SEEING YOU BOTH.

I THOUGHT YOU SAID HE WAS YOUR *FRIEND*.

I MIGHT HAVE BEEN OVERSTATING THINGS A BIT.

LYING, YOU MEAN.

LOOK-- *JUST* GIVE US A BITE TO EAT, AND GIVE US *TIME* TO FIGURE OUT WHERE WE'LL GO NEXT...

RRhrrrrhrhh...

NOW LOOK WHAT YOU'VE DONE--YOU'VE FRIGHTENED YO-YO!

COME BACK HERE, YOU STUPID BIRD!

HMPH!

HE WENT THROUGH THERE.

HELL!

WELL *WELL.* JASON *BLOOD,* ISN'T IT? HAVEN'T SEEN *YOU* IN A WHILE.

I AM SORRY. I CAN'T REMEMBER YOUR NAME.

JOHN CONSTANTINE.

"OH. YES, I REMEMBER YOU NOW. YOU WERE HANGED AT TYBURN, IN THE 1830s."

"NOT *ME,* SQUIRE. POSSIBLY SOMEONE ELSE WITH THE SAME NAME."

VERY LIKELY.

WE MET WHEN YOU WERE WORKING AS AN OCCULTIST IN GOTHAM, ABOUT TEN YEARS BACK. *REMEMBER?* I SAW YOU ABOUT THAT LUPUS BUSINESS.

NO.

SUIT YOURSELF.

...BUT IT WAS NIGHTTIME ALREADY! AND -- I MEAN THOSE *PEOPLE*...

I HAVE NO IDEA WHAT YOU'RE TALKING ABOUT!

ANOTHER CREATURE OF THE NIGHT, EH? WELL, WE ARE WELL-MATCHED. MY NAME IS JASON BLOOD.

HANG ON. JASON... *"IASON"?* YOU WERE WITH MERLIN. YOU'VE GOT THE SAME STREAKY HAIRSTYLE.

WE'VE MET BEFORE?

NOT REALLY.

I *WASN'T* PLANNING ON HOSTING A *DINNER PARTY*, CONSTANTINE.

THAT'S *GOOD*, COS I DIDN'T BRING A TUXEDO.

ARE YOU A *REAL* BARON?

SOMETIMES.

AH.

YOU WILL *EAT AND LEAVE*, DO YOU UNDERSTAND ME? YOU ARE *NOT* WELCOME HERE, CONSTANTINE.

TELL ME, BARON. ARE YOU GETTING *OUT* MUCH? *STILL* PART OF THE WASHINGTON SOCIAL WHIRL?

HMPH. YOUR ATTEMPTS AT HUMOR ARE AS PITIFUL AS EVER.

YOU SEE, TIM, THE BARON DOESN'T GO OUT. NOT OUT THE *FRONT* DOOR, AT ANY RATE. NOT INTO THE HERE AND NOW.

OH.

MIND IF I SMOKE, BARON?

TREMENDOUSLY.

SO, MR. BLOOD. TIM'S THINKING OF TAKING UP A CAREER IN MAGIC. YOU GOT ANY ADVICE FOR HIM?

DON'T DO IT. THE SHADOW-WORLD IS ALL GLAMOUR AND NO SUBSTANCE. AN *ILLUSION* OF BEAUTY AND POWER THAT COVERS A DEEP AND YAWNING ABYSS. AND AT THE *CORE* OF THAT ABYSS IS THE *PIT*, BOY.

AND YOU *DON'T* WANT TO GO TO *HELL,* BELIEVE ME.

YOU'RE HURTING MY HAND!

I'M SORRY.

S'OKAY.

NOW THEN, BARON. IT'S *YOUR* TURN. TELL THE KID ABOUT MAGIC.

YEAH. YOU MIGHT AS WELL. EVERYBODY *ELSE* HAS.

I KNOW NOTHING ABOUT MAGIC, CHILD. I WOULD SUSPECT IT TO BE A--

TIM.

I'M SORRY?

TIM, OR TIMOTHY. NOT CHILD. THAT *REALLY* GETS UP MY *NOSE,* THAT DOES.

IT IS STRANGE. I HAD PLANNED A *QUIET* DINNER WITH MR. BLOOD. WE WOULD HAVE CAUGHT UP ON CERTAIN CURRENT EVENTS; EXCHANGED INFORMATION; HAD A CIVILIZED MEAL, AND DISCUSSED DAYS GONE BY.

INSTEAD I FIND MYSELF ENTERTAINING AN INSIGNIFICANT LONDON HOODLUM WITH DELUSIONS OF WORLD-SAVING, AND HIS TRAVELING CIRCUS.

LEAVE IT OUT, BARON. TELL ME ABOUT THE MAGIC, AND THEN WE'LL TAKE OFF, AND YOU'LL *NEVER* HAVE TO SEE EITHER OF US AGAIN.

PROBABLY BECAUSE SOME *LOONY'LL* HAVE SLIT MY *THROAT.*

I HAVE *NO* IDEA WHY YOU SHOULD ASK ME... BUT IF IT WILL *HELP* TO SPEED YOUR DEPARTURE...

MAGIC IS *NOT IMPORTANT.* IT'S JUST CARD TRICKS. SHADOWS AND MIRRORS.

THEN WHAT *IS* IMPORTANT?

BEING WHO YOU ARE. SOLITUDE, IF THAT IS WHAT YOU CHOOSE. *CIVILIZA-TION. PRIVACY.*

TOMATO KETCHUP?

IN THE SILVER CONTAINER TO YOUR LEFT.

HE LIVES IN THE PAST, YOU KNOW.

YOU MEAN HE'S ALL ALONE IN THAT BIG HOUSE WITH HIS MEMORIES?

NAH. THE PAST IS WHERE HE DOES ALL HIS REAL LIVING.

WHO *IS* HE-- REALLY?

I DON'T KNOW. THAT'S ONE OF THE THINGS THAT HACKS ME OFF ABOUT HIM.

I SPENT *THREE WEEKS* ONCE, TRYING TO FIND OUT.

AND IN THREE WEEKS I CAN GET INTO *ANYTHING*; THE BANK OF ENGLAND VAULTS, OR A NUN'S KNICKERS.

GOT BUGGER ALL ON HIM, THOUGH.

GET IN.

THEY'RE STILL AFTER US, TIM. THE SOONER WE GET TO SAN FRANCISCO, THE HAPPIER I'LL BE.

÷YAHHN÷ MM. WHAT *HAPPENED*, JOHN? WHAT ARE WE GOING TO DO NOW?

STICK OUT OUR THUMBS, AND WALK, AND HOPE.

LOOK! FINALLY!

COME ON, JOHN --BEFORE HE CHANGES HIS MIND!

NOW, *HE* DOESN'T BELIEVE IN MAGIC.

AND HE'S *RIGHT.* MAGIC *DOESN'T* EXIST, FOR *HIM.*

YOU HAVE TO *CHOOSE* IT, YOU SEE. THAT'S WHAT WE'RE *OFFERING* YOU: THE CHOICE.

IF YOU *DON'T* WANT MAGIC, YOU'LL NEVER SEE IT AGAIN. YOU'LL LIVE IN A *RATIONAL* WORLD, IN WHICH *EVERYTHING* CAN BE EXPLAINED.

BUT IF YOU CHOOSE IT-- WELL, IT'S LIKE STEPPING OFF THE SIDEWALK INTO THE STREET.

THE WORLD STILL *LOOKS* THE SAME, ON THE SURFACE, BUT YOU CAN BE HIT BY A TRUCK AT ANY SECOND.

THAT'S MAGIC.

JOHN? I'M STARVING.

YOU CAN HAVE BREAKFAST AT OUR NEXT PORT OF CALL. AND SANCTUARY, TOO, WITH ANY LUCK.

WHERE ARE WE GOING NOW? *ANOTHER* ONE OF YOUR "OLD FRIENDS"?

AS IT HAPPENS, YES.

WHAT'S HIS NAME?

HER NAME. IT'S *ZATANNA.*

ZATANNA? THE *LADY MAGICIAN?* I'VE SEEN HER ON *TV* AND *EVERYTHING!* YOU KNOW HER? *WOW.*

AS IT HAPPENS, I USED TO KNOW HER QUITE WELL.

WHAT'S *THAT* MEANT TO MEAN?

OH. *OH DEAR.*

JUST THAT JUDGING BY THE WAY THINGS HAVE GONE SO FAR, SHE'LL BE A WEIRDO WHO HATES YOU.

NAH. ME AND ZATANNA, LIKE *THAT* WE ARE.

I EXPECT YOU PROBABLY *PINCHED* HER BEST TRICK, OR *KILLED* HER *BROTHER* OR SOMETHING.

FATHER.

I KILLED HER *FATHER*. OR AT LEAST, I WAS RESPONSIBLE FOR HIS DEATH.

WE WERE TRYING TO SAVE THE WORLD.

AND *DID* YOU?

GOD ALONE KNOWS, TIM.

AND EVEN HE'S PROBABLY STILL A LITTLE UNCERTAIN ABOUT THE FINAL OUTCOME...

THIS IS HER HOUSE.

ARE YOU SURE THIS IS A GOOD IDEA?

NO. BUT THE TRENCHCOAT BRIGADE WOULD NEVER TALK TO ME AGAIN IF WE GAVE UP NOW.

JOHN! *JOHN CONSTANTINE!*

JOHN, IT'S *WONDERFUL* TO SEE YOU! WHAT BRINGS YOU TO SAN FRANCISCO?

UM. HULLO ZATANNA.

COME ON IN. IT MUST BE WHAT, TWO YEARS? WHO'S YOUR FRIEND?

I'M TIM. TIMOTHY. TIMOTHY HUNTER. I *SAW YOU* ON JONATHAN ROSS.

THAT GUY WHO DOES LETTERMAN IN ENGLAND? YEAH, THAT WAS *FUN.* SO WHAT ARE YOU DOING HERE WITH MY OFF-WHITE KNIGHT, THEN?

TIM HAS THE *POTENTIAL* TO BE THE GREATEST MAGICIAN THAT THE MODERN WORLD HAS SEEN. SO ME, AND DOC OCCULT, AND THE STRANGER, AND THE NUT FROM BOSTON--

WHO?

HE CALLS HIMSELF MISTER E.

OH YEAH.

WELL, WE'VE GOT TOGETHER, AND WE'RE *SHOWING* HIM STUFF. THE *IDEA* IS THAT HE LEARNS *ENOUGH* ABOUT THE WORLD OF MAGIC TO DECIDE WHETHER *THAT'S* WHAT HE WANTS FROM LIFE OR NOT.

SOUNDS LIKE *FUN.*

ONLY TROUBLE IS, PEOPLE ARE TRYING TO *KILL* HIM.

SO WE'RE TRYING TO FIND SOMEWHERE TO HIDE UP THAT'S *SAFE,* UNTIL THE WHOLE THING BLOWS OVER.

WE *TRIED* BARON WINTER, BUT HE THREW US OUT.

WHY, OF *COURSE* YOU CAN STAY HERE! I'D BE *DELIGHTED* TO HAVE YOU. TIM CAN SLEEP IN THE SPARE BEDROOM...

OH--AND JOHN, THERE'S A LETTER FOR YOU ON THE TABLE OVER THERE.

A LETTER?

YEAH. THE ENVELOPE WAS THERE WHEN I CAME DOWN THIS MORNING. WEIRD, HUH?

GREAT LOOKING OWL, TIM. DID YOU MAKE HIM YOURSELF?

NO. DOCTOR OCCULT DID.

I COULDN'T BELIEVE IT WHEN YOU MADE THE FLOWERS GROW OUT OF JONATHAN ROSS'S EARS.

BUGGER. BLAST. DAMN. FELCHING HECK...

LOOK, TAKE CARE OF TIM UNTIL I GET BACK, CAN YOU LOVE?

BLOODY HELL.

HONESTLY! YOU CAN'T LEAVE THEM ALONE FOR *FIVE* MINUTES...

JOHN? WH-WHERE ARE YOU GOING?

INDIA. CALCUTTA, PROBABLY. SEEYA, DARLIN'. BYE, TIM.

INDIA? JOHN CONSTANTINE, YOU LIMEY DORK... OH, WHAT'S THE USE?

LOOK. I'M SORRY ABOUT THIS. I CAN GO.

NO. YOU'RE TWELVE, AND THEY'RE TRYING TO KILL YOU. WHEN DID YOU LAST EAT?

I'M NOT SURE. TRAVELING WITH HIM, TIME GOES REALLY FUNNY, IF YOU KNOW WHAT I MEAN.

MM. AND I DOUBT YOU'VE HAD A SHOWER SINCE YOU LEFT ENGLAND.

SO IF YOU HEAD UPSTAIRS YOU'LL FIND THE BATHROOM ON YOUR LEFT, AND I'LL HAVE BREAKFAST READY FOR YOU WHEN YOU COME DOWN.

YOU CAN LEAVE THE OWL WITH ME.

I'VE LEFT CLEAN CLOTHES OUTSIDE THE DOOR.

OKAY!

UM, THIS MAY BE A SILLY QUESTION, BUT WHERE DID YOU GET THE CLOTHES? IN MY SIZE?

MAGIC.

OH.

OKAY, I'VE MADE YOU BREAKFAST. IT'S VEGETARIAN, I'M AFRAID, BUT I THINK YOU'LL LIKE IT. YO-YO'S ASLEEP IN THE ATTIC FOR THE DAY.

HOW DID YOU KNOW HIS NAME'S YO-YO?

MAGIC.

OH.

THIS IS ABSOLUTELY INCREDIBLE. I WISH MY DAD COULD COOK LIKE THIS.

DID YOU MAKE THE FOOD BY MAGIC?

NO.

SAY-- IS THERE ANYONE YOU NEED TO PHONE?

I DUNNO. MAYBE I SHOULD RING MY DAD. I MEAN, JOHN SAID THEY'D TAKEN CARE OF ALL THAT. BUT I OUGHT TO LET HIM KNOW I'M OKAY.

HI, DAD.

TIM! HOW'S BRIGHTON?

I'M NOT IN BRIGHTON, DAD. I'M IN SAN FRANCISCO.

YEAH, IT'S RAINING HERE AS WELL. HOW'S YOUR AUNTIE BLODWYN, THEN? AND THE KIDS?

I'M IN SAN FRANCISCO, DAD. I'M STAYING WITH ZATANNA. YOU KNOW. THE MAGICIAN.

WELL, THAT'S GOOD. DON'T LOSE TOO MUCH MONEY ON THE SLOT MACHINES ON THE PIER. I KNOW HOW YOU LOVE THOSE THINGS. I'LL SEE YOU WHEN YOU GET BACK, THEN. CHEERS, LAD.

...BUT DAD."

HOW'S YOUR FATHER?

HE THINKS I'M IN BRIGHTON. I TOLD HIM I WASN'T, AND HE DIDN'T HEAR ME.

THIS IS REALLY WEIRD, YOU KNOW THAT? I MEAN, IT'S OKAY WHEN I'M WITH JOHN. WHEN YOU'RE WITH HIM THE WEIRD STUFF SEEMS ALMOST NORMAL.

PEOPLE FLYING. PEOPLE TRYING TO KILL ME.

IT'S JUST A BIG JOKE.

BUT NOW THAT HE'S GONE...

I SPOKE TO MY DAD, AND HE DIDN'T HEAR ME, ZATANNA.

I'M SCARED.

IT'S OKAY, TIM. IT'LL ALL BE FINE. DON'T WORRY.

YOU WANT TO LOOK AROUND THE CITY? YOU'RE UNDER MY PROTECTION, AND I WON'T LET ANY HARM COME TO YOU. I CAN SHOW YOU THE SIGHTS

YES, PLEASE.

ESOUH TCETORP FLESROUY.

WHAT DID YOU SAY?

I TOLD THE HOUSE TO PROTECT ITSELF. IN CASE ANYONE TRIES TO BREAK IN.

OH. IT SOUNDED LIKE YOU WERE TALKING BACKWARDS.

I *WAS*. IT'S HOW I WORK THE *ART. VERBALLY.* I TALK BACKWARDS.

IT'S MORE A *CONCENTRATION AID* THAN ANYTHING ELSE. MY FATHER USED TO DO IT, AND I SUPPOSE *I* GOT THE IDEA FROM *HIM*.

UM. LISTEN. IF IT'S A RUDE QUESTION YOU CAN TELL ME TO MIND MY OWN BUSINESS. BUT-- YOU AND JOHN CONSTANTINE. ARE *YOU*, UM...

NOT ANY MORE. NOT REALLY. NOT FOR A LONG TIME.

I DON'T THINK HE'S THE KIND FOR ANY KIND OF PERMANENT RELATIONSHIP. IF YOU SEE WHAT I MEAN.

YEAH. HE HASN'T EXACTLY STRUCK *ME* AS A PARTICULARLY PERMANENT PERSON, SO FAR.

WAIT HERE. I HAVE TO GO TO THE LADIES' ROOM.

TRICK OR TREAT?

TREAT, PLEASE.

SSHH. IT'S *ME*, KIDDO. *BOSTON BRAND*.

OH, HI.

SOME *HOT TOMATO*, HUH?

DOES THE WORD *"INCOMPREHENSIBLE"* MEAN ANYTHING TO YOU?

THAT ZATANNA. *OH, OH, OH*, WHAT A *GAL!* PLEASURES OF THE FLESH, HOW I MISS YA.

YOU'RE REALLY STARTING TO GET ON *MY NERVES*, MISTER BRAND. IF YOU DON'T MIND MY SAYING SO.

AFTER WHAT I DID FOR YOU *ALREADY?* I'VE SAVED YOUR LIFE *TWICE*, KIDDO.

YOU SHOULD THANK *GOD* THAT *SHE* KEPT ME AROUND AFTER I WAS SNUFFED. ANYWAY, I THOUGHT I'D LET YOU KNOW-- THE *SHINOLA'S* REALLY HIT THE FAN.

SPELLS, SACRIFICES, DEAD PEOPLE ALL OVER THE PLACE (ALTHOUGH *THAT'S* NOT REALLY ANYTHING NEW).

YOUR FRIEND *CONSTANTINE'S* RIGHT IN THE *MIDDLE* OF IT.

I THOUGHT HE WAS ON HIS WAY TO INDIA.

THAT'S WHERE IT'S ALL *HAPPENING*, KIDDO. IT'S HOT AND BLOODY AND *YOU'RE* THE KEWPIE DOLL PRIZE--

HI, GUYS.

UH...FEEL *DIZZY.* UM. *TWICK OR TWEAT?*

WELL, I DON'T HAVE ANY CANDY ON ME, BUT-- *OH!* WHAT'S THAT IN YOUR EAR?

WOW!

MAGIC?

I'M A STAGE MAGICIAN *TOO,* TIM. HIDE IN PLAIN SIGHT. IT'S THE ONLY WAY.

I...*SAW* YOUR FATHER. WHEN THE BLOKE IN THE BLACK HAT TOOK ME THROUGH THE PAST.

HE DIDN'T SEEM TO'VE HAD A VERY HAPPY LIFE.

NO. I DON'T THINK HE DID.

WE'D BETTER GET BACK.

WHERE ARE WE GOING?

WE'RE GOING TO A HALLOWE'EN PARTY.

WICKED! WHERE?

MM, I THOUGHT, SINCE JOHN WAS TRYING TO INTRODUCE YOU TO SOME OF THE MOST PROMINENT USERS OF MAGIC IN THE COUNTRY, I'D TAKE YOU OUT AND SHOW YOU A FEW *MORE* OF THEM...

BZZZT

OH, THERE'S THE CAB. I'LL BE DOWN IN A SEC.

YOU CALL FOR A *TAXI,* SIR?

NOT ME, BUT THE LADY DID. SHE'LL BE RIGHT DOWN.

TAA-DAA!

HOW DO I *LOOK?*

WELL, TIM. WHAT DO YOU THINK?

AREN'T YOU *EMBARRASSED?* DRESSED LIKE THAT?

NO. THIS WAS MY PROFESSIONAL OUTFIT, WHEN I WAS YOUNGER. IT'S KIND OF *FUN* TO WEAR IT EVERY NOW AND AGAIN. ANYWAY: IT'S HALLOWE'EN. C'MON.

THAT SCUZZBALL CONSTANTINE MAY NOT BE HERE. BUT *WE'LL* HAVE A GOOD TIME, WON'T WE?

WE'RE GOING TO A BAR CALLED *BEWITCHED.* ON HAIGHT AND FILLMORE. DO YOU *KNOW* IT?

YEAH. NEVER HAD ANYONE GO THERE BEFORE, THOUGH. SAY--

-- IS THE *BIRD* COMING TOO?

OF COURSE-- IT'S HALLOWE'EN.

NO PROBLEM. HAPPY HALLOWE'EN.

WE DON'T *HAVE* HALLOWE'EN IN ENGLAND. NOT LIKE YOU DO HERE. THAT'S WHAT *I* CALL MAGIC. *GHOSTS* AND *GHOULS* AND *WITCHES* AND *WEREWOLVES* WALKING THE STREETS...

IT'S LIKE CONSTANTINE SAID. IF YOU CAN *IMAGINE* IT, IT'S HERE *SOMEWHERE*.

WE'VE GOT *HISTORY*, BUT YOU'VE GOT *GEOGRAPHY*.

I'M SORRY, KID-- YOU *CAN'T* COME IN HERE. *SHOO*--AND TAKE THAT STUFFED BIRD *WITH* YOU!

YO-YO'S NOT *STUFFED.*

VERY FUNNY. ISN'T IT AFTER YOUR BED-TIME, SHORT STUFF?

HE'S WITH *ME*, APOLLONIUS. SO'S THE *OWL*.

WHY, MISS ZATANNA. THIS *IS* A WELCOME SURPRISE PLEASE, GO *IN*. I'M *SORRY*, CHILD, HAD I BUT *KNOWN*, YOU WERE WITH THE ENCHANTRESS...

YEAH.

I HAVEN'T COME DOWN HERE FOR *YEARS*. MAKES ME FEEL *YOUNG* AGAIN.

YOU DON'T LOOK OLD.

THANK YOU, YOUNG MAN. FOR THAT, YOU DESERVE A DRINK.

CAN I TAKE YOUR ORDER?

HELLO, TALA.

ZATANNA! NOBODY TOLD ME *YOU* WERE HERE! OH GAHD!

THIS IS MY FRIEND TIMOTHY, TALA. TALA, TIMOTHY.

TALA'S A QUEEN OF EVIL. SHE'S AN OLD ACQUAINTANCE OF YOUR FRIEND IN THE BLACK HAT, AND THE WHITE TURTLENECK.

HELLO, TALA.

HI, TIM. LISTEN, WE'RE GETTING KIND OF *BUSY*, NOW, BUT I'LL BE BACK TO *TALK* LATER. CAN I TAKE YOUR *ORDER?*

ICED WATER FOR ME. TIM?

CAN I HAVE A *SOUTHERN COMFORT?*

ONLY IF YOU CAN SHOW ME A GENUINE ID, PROVING YOU'RE OVER 21. *GINGER ALE?*

I SUPPOSE.

IF *SHE'S* THE QUEEN OF EVIL, WHY'S SHE WORKING *HERE?*

SHE'S JUST RESTING. BETWEEN ENGAGEMENTS, IF YOU SEE WHAT I MEAN. MOST OF THE PEOPLE IN HERE ARE IN A SIMILAR POSITION.

COME ON.

TANNARAK--THIS IS TIM HUNTER.

TANNARAK WANTS TO LIVE FOREVER. HE'S ANOTHER ONE OF THE BAD GUYS. A BLACK MAGICIAN. HE ALSO *OWNS* THIS CLUB.

DELIGHTFUL AS USUAL, ZATANNA. CHARMED TO MAKE YOUR ACQUAINTANCE, YOUNG MAN. HAVE YOU ANY REQUESTS? ANYTHING YOU WANT TO KNOW?

YES. UM, ARE YOU REALLY A BLACK MAGICIAN?

CERTAINLY NOT.

THERE'S NO SUCH *THING* AS BLACK MAGIC. IT'S SEMANTIC DRIFT.

BLACK MAGIC IS A TRANSLATION OF THE WORD *NIGROMANCY*, YOU SEE. AND NIGROMANCY IS JUST A CORRUPTION OF "NECROMANCY." *THE MAGIC OF THE DEAD.*

IT'S NOT *BLACK* MAGIC VERSUS *WHITE* MAGIC. I TEND TO THINK OF IT AS *LIVE* MAGIC VERSUS *DEAD* MAGIC. BUT EVEN *THAT'S* SIMPLISTIC DUALISM...

ADDITIONALLY, MAGIC, EVEN DARK MAGIC, *ISN'T* SATANISM -- ALTHOUGH I'VE DEALT WITH THE ODD DEVIL IN MY TIME. *MAGIC* IS ABOUT *POWER*. IT'S SEEING *THROUGH* THE SHADOWS TO THE REAL *WORLD* BEYOND.

I SEE. I THINK. AND TANNARAK ISN'T YOUR REAL NAME, IS IT?

NAMES HAVE *POWER*, CHILD. YOU LEARN FAST. WHY DON'T YOU TAKE A LOOK AROUND?

UM. I JUST *REALIZED* SOMETHING. THE PEOPLE HERE. NONE OF THEM ARE WEARING MASKS, ARE THEY?

NO.

IT'S LIKE THERE'S A WHOLE OTHER *WORLD*, THAT I NEVER KNEW *EXISTED*, SIDE BY SIDE WITH THE OLD ONE.

YES. AND ONCE YOU ENTER IT, YOU CAN NEVER LEAVE.

NEVER?

YOU HAVEN'T ENTERED IT YET, TIM. YOU'RE A GUEST.

CALL YOURSELF AN *ENCHANTER?* YOU COULDN'T TURN A FROG INTO A, ER, INTO ANOTHER FROG. A DIFFERENT ONE.

AND *YOU COULD,* I SUPPOSE, *WIZARD?*

I HAVE MORE MAGIC IN MY *NAVEL FLUFF* THAN YOU DO IN YOUR ENTIRE BODY.

IF YOU WISH TO STEP *OUTSIDE,* FAUST, WE CAN SETTLE THIS LIKE *GENTLEMEN* OF THE *ART.*

UH, NO, *NO,* I DON'T NEED TO PROVE ANYTHING TO *YOU.*

HE CALLS HIMSELF *FELIX FAUST.* GIVES ME THE CREEPS. CLAIMS TO BE *THOUSANDS* OF YEARS OLD; BUT HE *LIES* A LOT, AND I *THINK* HE WAS LYING ABOUT THAT.

THE *OTHER* CALLS HIMSELF *THE WIZARD.* I SUPPOSE HE WAS MY *FATHER'S* OPPOSITE NUMBER, YEARS AGO.

ONE OF THE BAD GUYS.

IT WOULD BE *NICE* TO THINK THAT HIS LIFE HAD BEEN RUINED BY EVIL... THAT MY FATHER'S LIFE WAS HAPPY WHILE THE WIZARD'S IS A SOUR, TIRED THING.

BLACK MAGIC VERSUS WHITE, ALL THAT.

AND?

I DON'T *KNOW,* TIMOTHY...

HEY-- KIDDO. GET *OUT* OF HERE.

WHAT?

IT'S *ME*-- BOSTON BRAND.

I DUNNO, SOMEHOW I'M NOT SURPRISED.

THAT STUFF I WAS TELLING YOU ABOUT BEFORE-- YOU WOULDN'T BE*LIEVE* IT. THE CULT OF KALI, THREE NINJA DEATH SQUADS, THE BROTHER-HOOD OF THE COLD FLAME, A *THOUSAND* ELEPHANTS...

THE STRANGER, DOC OCCULT, CONSTANTINE, THE LOONEY TUNE --ALL OF THEM. *MAJOR* OCCULT BATTLE. *BLOOD. DEVASTATION. WEIRD* STUFF LIKE YOU WOULDN'T *BELIEVE.*

HUH?

I *THINK* IT'S ALL OVER BAR THE SCREAM-ING. BUT I JUST *OVERHEARD...*

--GET *OUT OF MY HEAD!*--

I DON'T *BELIEVE* IT--

-- LEAVE, I ABJURE THEE! 'EASFYSHUE ORPSS 'I TSCASRPOI NU ?'MELN, DMYLTCRIOS 'RE IHODSAYUR 'UN H'TGAH--

--YOW!--

PADPUKS-TOGASSO HRYFOTLO-SRVLIG AEI OKHIYAD-SIYA.

FRIGGIN' SPOOKS.

LADIES. GENTLEMEN. OTHER ENTITIES. I HAVE AN ANNOUNCEMENT.

IT SEEMS THERE'S A VERY *SPECIAL* YOUNG LAD IN OUR AUDIENCE TONIGHT.

SOME OF YOU MAY HAVE *HEARD* ABOUT HIM, ON THE *GRAPEVINE*. OTHERS OF YOU MIGHT HAVE HEARD ABOUT THE *CURRENT* FUN AND GAMES IN *CALCUTTA*.

OH, *SHOOT*. I'M SORRY, TIM -- I SHOULD *NEVER* HAVE BROUGHT YOU HERE.

AS YOU KNOW THERE *IS* A *PRICE* ON HIS *HEAD*--WHICH NEED NOT BE ATTACHED TO HIS *BODY*.

THIS BOY IS UNDER *MY* PROTECTION. *ANYONE* WHO WISHES TO HURT *HIM* MUST FIRST RECKON WITH *ME*.

MY *DEAR* ZATANNA. FACE *FACTS*--THERE'S *ONE* OF YOU, AND OVER A *HUNDRED* OF US.

THE CHILD IS *HISTORY*.

GER OU' OGH DHA RAY, ZHACHANNA...

I AM THE MISTRESS OF ALL MIRRORS, WOMAN. GIVE ME THE BOY, OR ONE NIGHT YOUR REFLECTION WILL SNEAK OUT OF ITS FRAME AND CUT YOUR SLEEPING THROAT.

COME HERE, LITTLE BOY. COME TO HYACINTH AND LEANDER. GOOD BOY. LITTLE BOY. COME HERE.

CONSTANTINE.

NOBODY TOUCHES THAT BOY.

THAT'S RIGHT.

THE BOY'S *MINE.* AND IN THIRTY SECONDS, ME, AND HIM, AND THE WITCH, ARE GOING TO WALK OUT OF HERE.

YOU KNOW WHO I AM. OR YOU *OUGHT* TO.

YOU KNOW MY REPUTATION. NOW...

...DOES ANYONE HERE *REALLY* WANT TO START SOMETHING?

RIGHT. COME ON, YOU LOT. WE'RE LEAVING.

I *COULD* HAVE STOPPED THEM, YOU KNOW.

YEAH. YOU PROBABLY COULD.

JOHN, YOU *DON'T* HAVE ANY POWER TO SPEAK OF. ANY*ONE* OF THEM COULD HAVE TORN YOU TO *SHREDS.*

BUT THEY... WERE *SCARED* OF YOU.

I DON'T UNDERSTAND WHAT *HAPPENED* BACK THERE.

MAGIC.

NO, *SERIOUSLY,* JOHN...

A *GOOD* MAGICIAN *NEVER* TELLS YOU HOW HE DID A TRICK, LOVE. *YOU* TAUGHT ME THAT. BUT IT *HELPS* THAT THEY'RE ALL A FEW GUPPIES SHORT OF AN AQUARIUM.

SPEAK *ENGLISH,* CAN'T YOU?

I SPEAK *PERFECT* ENGLISH. SO DOES *TIM.* IT'S *YOU* THAT'S GOT THE *FUNNY ACCENT.*

WHAT HAPPENED TO YOUR FACE?

YOU WOULDN'T BELIEVE ME IF I TOLD YOU.

MISTER CONSTANTINE-- ARE YOU MYSTERIOUS ABOUT *EVERYTHING?*

WHO? *ME?* MYSTERIOUS? TRANSPARENT AS *GLASS,* I AM...

TIM. IT WAS *GREAT* MEETING YOU. CALL ME THE NEXT TIME YOU'RE IN THE STATES. OKAY?

'COURSE. YOU'VE BEEN *TERRIFIC*. THANKS FOR EVERYTHING.

NO PROBLEM. YOU WERE A GREAT HOUSE-GUEST.

NOW, JOHN CONSTANTINE... I DON'T THINK I'LL *EVER* UNDERSTAND YOU. NOT IF I LIVE TO BE A *THOUSAND*.

NO? SORRY ABOUT THAT. GIVE US A *KISS* AND I'LL BE OUT OF YOUR LIFE FOR ANOTHER YEAR OR SO.

BY THE WAY. I ALMOST FORGOT. *WE* HAVEN'T GOT *PASSPORTS* OR *TICKETS*, UM. COULD YOU, Y'KNOW, TWITCH YOUR NOSE OR SOMETHING?

JERK. STROPSSAP DNA STEKCIT REAPPA.

SO EVERYTHING'S *COPACETIC*, HUH, *KIDDO*?

HULLO, MISTER BRAND. IT *IS* YOU, ISN'T IT? YOU *STILL* AREN'T MAKING ANY SENSE.

NO PROBLEM. IT'S BEEN *FUN*. I'LL PROBABLY SEE YOU *AROUND* SOMETIME.

I'M *SORRY*. I THINK I BLACKED OUT FOR A SECOND. *HEADPHONES?*

NO, THANK YOU.

OK -- SO WHAT HAVE YOU LEARNED?

LEARNED?

YEAH. COME ON. I'VE DRAGGED YOU *HALFWAY* AROUND THE *WORLD;* YOU'VE BEEN INTRODUCED TO, INSULTED, OR *THREATENED* BY SOME OF THE MOST POWERFUL PRACTITIONERS OF THE ART IN EXISTENCE.

WHAT HAVE YOU *LEARNED?*

I DUNNO. THAT ALL OF THEM EXCEPT ZATANNA ARE ABOUT AS *WELL-BALANCED* AS UPTURNED *EGGS.*

YEAH -- THAT'S A GOOD BEGINNING.

AND THAT THEY DON'T LIVE IN THE SAME *WORLD* THAT MOST PEOPLE DO.

THEIR WORLD IS LIKE A *SHADOW* OF OURS. DARK AND DISTORTED, BUT STILL *CONNECTED...*

AM I MAKING *SENSE?*

MORE THAN YOU KNOW.

DR. OCCULT WILL BE WAITING FOR YOU WHEN WE LAND IN *GATWICK. HE'LL* BE YOUR GUIDE FOR THE *NEXT* LEG OF THE TRIP.

OH. WHERE'S *HE* GOING TO TAKE ME, THEN? *MANCHURIA? TIBET? OUTER SPACE?*

FAIRYLAND.

FAIRYLAND?

Scott Hampton
10-31-90

Book III: The Land of Summer's Twilight

POSSIBLY.

YOU FOUR. WHO ARE YOU? I MEAN, CONSTANTINE, HE'S JUST A BLOKE, ISN'T HE?

JOHN CONSTANTINE...

WILL YOU TELL ME SOMETHING?

YES. HE DANCES ON THE EDGE OF THE KNOWN, LIKE A CRAZY MAN, PITTING HIMSELF AGAINST HEAVEN AND THE PIT, BECAUSE HE IS JOHN CONSTANTINE; AND BECAUSE HE IS ALIVE.

HOW ABOUT MISTER E? IS HE REALLY BLIND?

OH YES. HE...HE IS AN EXTREMIST. HE FIGHTS WHAT HE SEES AS THE FORCES OF DARKNESS; BUT SOMETIMES I SUSPECT THAT ALL HE EVER CAN SEE IS DARKNESS...

HOWEVER, HE CAN TRAVEL WAYS THAT EVEN I CANNOT.

AND THE OTHER ONE? HE SPOOKS ME...

THE STRANGER? AHH. I HAVE ENCOUNTERED HIM, MANY TIMES, IN THE PAST. HE ALSO WALKS HIS OWN PATH. ONE THAT BEGAN TOO LONG AGO, AND I SUSPECT, HAS NO END IN VIEW.

I DO NOT KNOW HIS STORY. I KNOW NO ONE WHO DOES; ALTHOUGH I HAVE HEARD CONJECTURES APLENTY: THAT HE IS THE WANDERING JEW, OR AN ANGEL WHO NEITHER FELL WITH LUCIFER NOR FOUGHT AT MICHAEL'S SIDE, OR...

THERE ARE OTHER GUESSES.

SOME SAY HE OWES ALLEGIANCE TO ORDER, OR TO CHAOS, OR TO BALANCE: SPECULATIONS ALL. I DO NOT KNOW WHAT HE IS. AND PERHAPS HE HAS WALKED TO FORGET SO LONG THAT HE HIMSELF NO LONGER REMEMBERS.

AH. AND HOW ABOUT YOU?

I AM YOUR *GUIDE* THROUGH THIS STAGE OF YOUR JOURNEY, TIMOTHY HUNTER. AND YOU MAY *TRUST* ME.

EMPTY YOUR POCKETS.

LEAVE THE *KEYS* AND THE *COINS* HERE-- TIE THEM IN YOUR KERCHIEF, PERHAPS. *COLD IRON* WILL NOT BE WELCOME WHERE WE GO. THE REST YOU MAY *RETAIN*.

LISTEN TO ME *CAREFULLY*, NOW. THERE ARE THINGS YOU MUST REMEMBER.

FIRSTLY, ON OUR JOURNEY, YOU MUST OBEY MY ORDERS *EXPLICITLY* AND IN *ALL* THINGS, NO MATTER HOW *PETTY* OR *STRANGE* THEY SEEM TO YOU.

SECONDLY, ASK NO *QUESTIONS* OR *FAVORS* OF THOSE YOU MEET ON OUR TRAVELS; AND *ACCEPT NO GIFTS*, OR *FOOD-STUFFS*, OR *FAVORS*, SAVE WITH MY BLESSING.

THIRDLY, REMEMBER YOUR *MANNERS*: ETIQUETTE WILL BE *IMPORTANT* WHERE WE GO, AND *GOOD MANNERS* ARE GOLD.

FOR A TRIVIAL IMPOLITENESS YOU COULD FIND YOURSELF *GIFTED* WITH *ASSES' EARS*, OR *WORSE*.

LASTLY, *NEVER* STRAY FROM THE PATH. NO MATTER *WHAT* YOU SEE, OR HEAR, OR FEEL.

DO YOU *UNDERSTAND*?

I SUPPOSE SO.

GOOD.

THEN WE ARE READY TO BEGIN OUR JOURNEY.

WAIT HERE. I WILL WALK ACROSS TO THAT WICKET GATE. WHEN I *WAVE* TO YOU, THEN WALK AS I WALKED, ALONG THAT PATH. WHEN YOU CROSS THE *STREAM* BEFORE THE GATE, TAKE CARE NOT TO GET YOUR FEET WET. *YES*?

FINE.

YO-YO? *WHY* ARE WE DOING THIS? I MEAN, WHY AM I *DOING* THIS STUFF? *ANYONE* WITH HALF AN OUNCE OF SENSE WOULD HAVE TOLD THEM *ALL* TO *BUGGER OFF* AT THE *BEGINNING...*

OH WELL. TOO LATE NOW.

HERE GOES!

RIGHT. I'M HERE. UM... DOCTOR?

YES.

CONSTANTINE SAID WE WERE GOING TO *FAIRYLAND*. HE *WAS* KIDDING, WASN'T HE?

WE TRAVEL THROUGH THE FAIR LANDS, CHILD. CALL THEM *AVALON*, OR *ELVENHOME*, OR *DOM-DANIEL*, OR *FAERIE*, IT MATTERS NOT. IT IS THE LAND OF SUMMER'S TWILIGHT.

OH. SO WHEN DO WE GO THERE?

LOOK *BEHIND* YOU, CHILD.

108

OH.

NO. I AM NO LONGER DOCTOR OCCULT, ALTHOUGH WE SHARE CERTAIN *PURPOSES* IN COMMON. *HE* IS *HIMSELF*, AS *I* AM *ME*. BUT I AM *STILL YOUR GUIDE.*

UM. GOSH. IS THAT WHAT YOU *REALLY* LOOK LIKE?

I DON'T *UNDERSTAND...*

MALE AND *FEMALE.* ANIMUS AND ANIMA.

THESE ARE THINGS WE CARRY *WITHIN* OURSELVES. IN *THIS* ASPECT I AM *FEMALE.* IT MAKES CERTAIN THINGS... *EASIER.*

WHAT'S YOUR...? I MEAN, *PLEASE*, WHAT ARE YOU *CALLED?*

FIND A NAME FOR ME.

FIND ONE?

THAT'S RIGHT.

A *NAME?*

IT'S A *TEST*, OF SORTS.

I BET IT'S BLOODY *RUMPEL-STILTSKIN.*

THAT'S *GOOD*, TIM. AND *FAST.* THE STRANGER WAS *RIGHT*--YOU HAVE THE *POTENTIAL* FOR POWER.

I'LL CALL YOU *ROSE.*

SO WHERE ARE WE OFF TO NOW, THEN?

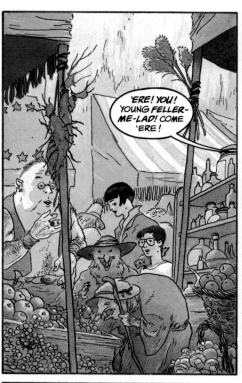

'ERE! YOU! YOUNG FELLER-ME-LAD! COME 'ERE!

I'LL *SWOP* YOU YER *HEART'S DESIRE* FER A YEAR OF YER LIFE. *NO?* YER *VOICE*, THEN? OR THE *COLOR* OF YER *EYES?*

NO, THANK YOU.

ONE OF YER *FINGERS*, THEN. YER'VE GOT *TEN* OF THE LITTEL BUGGERS, YOU'LL *NEVER* MISS ONE. IT'S YER *HEART'S DESIRE* I'M OFFRIN', DUCKY, NONE OF YER *TAT*.

ALL RIGHT, *TWO* TOES, AND *SIX* MONTHS OF YOUR OLD AGE FOR YOUR HEART'S DESIRE, AND *THAT'S* ME FINAL OFFER.

NO THANKS. BUT *THANKS* ANYWAY.

YOU'VE GOT A *GOOD HEART*, DEARIE. HERE -- LET ME GIVE YOU A *GIFT*. A FLASK OF *BEST BERRY-JUICE* FOR YER JOURNEY.

I MUST THANK YOU FOR THE OFFER, MISTRESS, BUT ALSO *DECLINE* IT.

THE BOY IS UNDER MY PROTECTION, AND CANNOT DALLY AMONGST THE FAIR FOLK.

FAIR *SPOKEN*, LADY. I WISH YOU *GOOD TRAVELING*, AND THAT'S FOR *FREE*.

WHAT HAVE WE HERE?

THIS *BIRD* OF YOURS *ATTACKED* ME! I DEMAND COMPENSATION!

112

YO-YO? IS THIS *TRUE?*

WHOO.

IT *SAYS* YOU WERE TRYING TO PUT THAT BRACELET IN TIMOTHY'S POCKET. IT *SAW* YOU, AND STOPPED YOU.

RUBBISH! IT WAS AN *UNPROVOKED* ATTACK! BUT I HAVE THOUGHT *BETTER* OF DEMANDING COMPENSATION, AND WILL BE *CONTENT* TO LET THE MATTER REST HERE.

YOU MAY BE. *I* AM NOT. WHERE IS THE WARDEN OF THE MARKET?

OH, *DON'T* BOTHER OLD GLORY WITH THIS. GLORY *HATES* TO BE BOTHERED WITH MARKET AFFAIRS...

MARKET AFFAIRS ARE GLORY'S *BUSINESS* AS WARDEN, SNOUT. *AS* ARE ITS *TRADERS.*

SO. YOU WOULD HAVE *PLANTED* THE TORQUE IN THE CHILD'S POCKET, WAITED UNTIL HE WAS ABOUT TO LEAVE THE MARKET, THEN SHOUTED *"STOP THIEF!"*

AND AS WRONGED PARTY, *YOU* WOULD HAVE BEEN ENTITLED TO HAVE THE BOY BE YOUR *PERSONAL SERVANT* FOR *SEVENTY* YEARS. *AND* TO CLAIM RESTITUTION FROM HIS COMPANIONS INTO THE BARGAIN...

113

SILENCE.

ER, LORD GLORY...

YOU ARE EVIDENTLY THE WRONGED PARTIES HERE, AND I REGRET THAT SNOUT'S ACTION HAS TARNISHED THE NAME OF THE MARKET.

YOU MAY CLAIM RESTITUTION. HMMM.

SNOUT, LEAD US TO YOUR BARROW.

NOW THEN, SNOUT: THE BOY, THE WOMAN, AND THE OWL. EACH OF THESE YOU WOULD HAVE WRONGED.

AS MARKET WARDEN THIS IS MY JUDGMENT: EACH OF THEM MAY TAKE, FREE, GRATIS, AND WITHOUT OBLIGATION, ONE ITEM FROM YOUR BARROW.

AT **LEAST** WE DIDN'T HAVE TO WADE THROUGH IT FOR FORTY DAYS AND FORTY NIGHTS...

A **SEA** OF **BLOOD?** WHY?

WHY? THAT'S A STRANGE QUESTION.

PERHAPS BECAUSE THERE IS SOME LEVEL ON WHICH WE ARE **SITTING** ON A **HILLSIDE** IN SUSSEX, **EXPLORING** A WORLD **INSIDE** OURSELVES.

PERHAPS BECAUSE IT'S A METAPHOR FOR **WOMAN'S POWER,** FOR **FERTILITY** AND **MYSTERY.**

AND PERHAPS BECAUSE THIS IS **NO** METAPHOR: WE'RE IN FAERIE, AND **THIS** IS WHAT HAPPENS IN FAERIE.

IT DIDN'T FEEL LIKE A **METATHINGIE** TO ME. IT WAS **HORRIBLE.**

UECH! IT'S DIS-**GUSTING.** CAN'T YOU **MAGIC** IT AWAY?

NO.

BUT--

IT WILL DRY SOON, AND VANISH. NOTHING IN THIS PLACE LASTS FOREVER, TIM.

GREAT. JUST GREAT.

AT LEAST WITH **CONSTANTINE** ALL I HAD TO WORRY ABOUT WAS PEOPLE TRYING TO KILL ME.

WHERE ARE WE?

I DO NOT KNOW. THIS PATH HAS NEVER LED ME TO THIS PLACE BEFORE.

LET'S GO SOMEWHERE **ELSE,** THEN...

WE **MUST** STAY ON THE PATH, TIMOTHY. ONCE WE HAVE BEGUN TO WALK OUR ROAD, WE **MUST** WALK IT **ALL** THE WAY. OR WE ARE **LOST.**

AND **ALL** MAY BE LOST.

A *RIDDLE GAME*?

WHAT'S HAPPENING? WHAT'S GOING ON?

VERY WELL. BUT ONE RIDDLE ONLY. I WILL ASK AND YOU WILL ANSWER.

LATER.

VERY WELL. ASK YOUR RIDDLE.

WHEN THERE IS FIRE IN ME THEN I AM STILL COLD; WHEN I OWN YOUR TRUE LOVE'S FACE THEN YOU WILL NOT SEE ME;

TO ALL THINGS I GIVE NO MORE THAN I AM GIVEN; IN TIME I MAY HAVE ALL THINGS, AND YET I CAN KEEP NOTHING.

ER...

WOULD YOU MIND *REPEATING* THAT?

I HAVE STATED MY RIDDLE. SOLVE IT, AND ENTER, OR FAIL, AND DIE.

A *MIRROR*?

ENTER, THEN.

SO HEARKEN TO THE SONG I SING
OF KINGS BENEATH THE HILL:
FOR EVERY NATION HAS ITS KING
WHO SLEEPS BENEATH A HILL.
AND IN ITS TIME OF GREATEST PAIN
HE'LL WAKE, AND WAR, PREVAIL, AND REIGN,
AND HAPPY DAYS ARE HERE AGAIN...
BUT FOR NOW HE SLEEPS UNDER THE HILL--
THE HILL--
FOR LEGENDS ARE BUGGERS TO KILL.

THE LORD BE PRAISED. AN *AUDIENCE*. WELL, WELL. TRUE MORTALS, BY THE LOOK OF YE.

IT'S BEEN A *LONG* TIME SINCE I'VE HAD COMPANY BENEATH THE HILL.

I AM *SURPRISED* THAT MAUGYS ALLOWED YE THROUGH SO EASILY.

MAUGYS?

THE *GIANT* AT THE *DOOR*.

WE HAD A *RIDDLE* GAME, AND I SOLVED THE RIDDLE AND *BESTED* HIM.

NO YOU *DIDN'T*. IT WAS A TOTAL *FLUKE*. YOU DIDN'T EVEN *GUESS*. HE JUST *THOUGHT* YOU DID.

AH, THAT *MIGHT* BE HOW IT *LOOKED*. HOWEVER--

LISTEN, IF YOU *REALLY* THINK--

GENTLEMEN. *GENTLEMEN*. SHOULD WE NOT *INTRODUCE* OURSELVES? I AM CALLED *THOMAS*.

TIMOTHY. TIM HUNTER.

I AM KNOWN AS--

I *KNOW* THEE *NOW*, *MELCHIOR*. WE MET WHEN I WAS *STILL* LIVING *ABOVE* THE EARTH. DOST THOU NOT *REMEMBER* ME?

I THINK NOT.

121

TRUE THOMAS, THEY CALLED ME. *RHYMING* THOMAS. *YES?* YE CAME TO *ERCELDOUN*, WHEN I WAS EIGHTEEN, AND THE *VILLAGE* WAS PLAGUED BY *WHITE TOADS* THAT *SANG* IN THE *DUSK* OF A *LADY* WHOSE *LOVE* WAS A *WORM...*

THERE WAS A *MAIDEN* WITH THEE. *ROSE*, HER NAME WAS, AND I TUMBLED HER *ONCE*, BENEATH THE *STARS* ON A BED OF CUT BRACKEN.

SIX HUNDRED YEARS HAVE GONE SINCE THEN. BUT IF *STILL* SHE LIVES I *THINK* SHE'D REMEMBER ME.

I DOUBT IT.

PERHAPS NOT. IT WAS *LONG AGO.*

BUT *THINE* IS THE *QUEST*, YOUNG MASTER. *WHAT* WOULDST THOU KNOW, WITH AN *OWL* ON THY SHOULDER AND AN *EGG* IN THY *POCKET?*

UM. *I* DUNNO. WELL, WHAT *IS* THIS PLACE, FOR A START? AND *WHO* IS HE?

THIS PLACE IS *JOYOUS GARD*, AND HE IS THE *KING.*

THE KING OF *THIS* PLACE?

NO, LADDIE. HE'S A KING OF *THY* WORLD. HE'S THE KING WHO SLEEPS BENEATH THE HILL.

IN *HIS COUNTRY'S* TIME OF *GREATEST TRAVAIL*, HE'LL RISE AND DEFEAT ITS OPPRESSORS.

122

WHERE ARE YOU?

HERE.

WHERE?

NOW, *WHAT'S* BABA YAGA CAUGHT FOR HERSELF, THEN?

YOU BETTER LET ME *GO.* DOCTOR OCCULT IS MY PROTECTOR. *HE'LL* FIND YOU. YOU'LL BE IN *BIG* TROUBLE.

FIND US? I *DOUBT* IT, MANLING.

IS IT A *STEW?*

IS IT A *ROAST?*

IS IT *BLOOD PUDDING?*

IS IT *TENDER CUTLETS?*

OH YES. ALL OF THEM. *JUICY* AND *MEATY* AND *TOOTH-SOME* AND *SWEET.*

BABA YAGA'S LITTLE *HOUSE* IS IN THE *HEART* OF THE WILD FOREST. AND IT WILL *NOT* BE FOUND IN THE *SAME PLACE* TWO DAYS RUNNING...

NOW, MY HOUSE, DO YOU GO *WANDERING.*

"THERE'S MEAT ON THOSE RIBS. *GOOD.*

"STEAK ON THAT RUMP. *GOOD.*

"AND *HEART,* TO *CHEW.*

"AND *EYES* TO SUCK.

"AND *TONGUE* TO *BOIL,* AND EAT *PIPING HOT.* "

I REALLY think you ought to LET ME GO, you know.

I'LL BE BACK SOON, MY JUICY.

BABA YAGA needs VEGETABLES, YES, and HERBS, and KINDLING.

OHH. SUCH FEASTING I WILL MAKE. THE GREASE WILL RUN DOWN MY CHIN, AND I WILL CRACK YOUR BONES WITH MY IRON TEETH, TO SUCK THE MARROW FROM WITHIN...

WINDOW! OPEN YOU WIDE!

You've DONE it this time, matey.

WHAT?

He's RIGHT, you know. You're goin' to be STEW.

I mean, ME and Master REDLAW here, we're fairly USED to the idea of endin' up in the cookpot.

So to speak, Master Leveret, although MOSTLY us hedge-pigs is encased in clay and roasted in embers, 'cos of us havin' us's PRICKLES.

Stands corRECTED, Master Redlaw. Stands corrected and grateful to yer, I MUS' say.

UM...

WELL, YO-YO, IF YOU SEE DR. OCCULT AGAIN, TELL HIM I'M *SORRY* I STEPPED OFF THE PATH. AND THAT I *WISH* I'D NEVER *STARTED* ON THIS MAGIC STUFF.

AND TELL HIM TO SAY *GOODBYE* TO DAD FOR ME.

RIGHT?

WHOO.

It said, fair enough.

You know, there is a remarkable pe*CULiar THING* about yon hooty-owl.

You mean it bein' out in the daytime, when everybody knows Owls is night-time folks?

Why, that's exceedin' perspicious of you. But *NO*, what I was thinkin' was more in the nature of the chain wrapped *AROUND* itself that was out of the ordinary.

IT'S *JUST* A CHAIN WE GOT AT THE GOBLIN MARKET. YO-YO GOT IT FROM A *BARROW*.

"JUST A CHAIN?" That's *EMPUSA'S INFINITELY EXTENSIBLE,* that is, or as near as makes no damn-it (if you'll pardon my french).

Now *THERE'S* a thing, Master Redlaw! Empusa's Infinitely Extensible Chain, a-wrapped around an *OWL*.

WHAT ARE YOU *TALKING* ABOUT?

FAMOUS it is, matey. One of Empusa's lost treasures, right up there with the *DRUM UNESCAPABLE,* and the *HELIOTROPE GAMAHAEAN UNION.*

"Well, paint me pink and call me a noodle, Master Redlaw, if I didn't com*PLETELY* miss the point of what you was gettin' at earlier. You must think me a *RIGHT* old puddin'-head!"

"Think *NUFFINK* of it, Master Leveret. Us hedgeypiggles is natural born thinkers."

SO... IS *THIS* GOING TO GET US *DOWN?*

NO, laddie. *NO*, I can't with all honesty say that it *WILL*.

But it's *DEFINITE* summat to tell yer *GRANDCHILDREN*, eh, Master Redlaw? "Coincidentally, the werry same day I was popped into a cook-pot, I discovered Empusa's Infinitely Extensible Chain, on a owl."

Although, *THAT* bein' said...

132

OUT OF MY *WAY,* WOMAN. THAT *BRAT* IS MY *DINNER*-- AND HE'S HURT MY LITTLE *HOUSE!*

TIMOTHY IS UNDER *MY* PROTECTION IN THIS REALM. I CHARGE YOU TO TROUBLE HIM NO *MORE.*

HE'S *MINE!* AND YOU DARE *THREATEN* ME? WHY, *I* SHOULD...

I KNOW YOUR *TRUE* NAME, BABA YAGA.

DO YOU WISH ME TO *SHOUT* IT *NOW,* SO THAT ALL THE *ANIMALS* OF THE *FOREST,* ALL THE *BIRDS* OF THE *AIR,* EVERY PASSING *NIXIE* AND *BOGGART* WILL KNOW IT TOO?

YOUR *NAME* WILL BE COMMON AS CRAB-GRASS.

WOULD YOU *LIKE* THAT, BABA YAGA?

YOU'RE *LYING.* YOU *DO* NOT KNOW MY *NAME.*

PERHAPS. DO YOU WISH TO FIND OUT HOW *LOUDLY* I CAN *SHOUT?*

...NO.

THEN DO YOU *DISCHARGE* ALL *OBLIGATION* AND LIEN ON THE BOY?

...I DO.

GOOD.

133

NO, TIMOTHY. *NOT* FAR.

YOU WISH TO SEE THE DISTANT REALMS? VERY WELL.

BUT KNOW THIS FIRST: THE PLACES YOU WILL VISIT, THE PLACES THAT YOU WILL SEE, *DO NOT EXIST.*

FOR THERE ARE ONLY *TWO* WORLDS -- *YOUR* WORLD, WHICH IS THE *REAL* WORLD, AND *OTHER* WORLDS, THE *FANTASY.*

WORLDS LIKE *THIS* ARE WORLDS OF THE HUMAN IMA- GINATION: THEIR *REALITY*, OR *LACK* OF REALITY, IS NOT IMPORTANT. WHAT *IS* IMPORTANT IS THAT THEY ARE *THERE.*

THESE WORLDS PROVIDE AN *ALTERNATIVE.* PROVIDE AN *ESCAPE.* PROVIDE A *THREAT.* PROVIDE A *DREAM*, AND *POWER*, PROVIDE *REFUGE*, AND *PAIN.*

THEY GIVE *YOUR WORLD* MEANING.

THEY DO *NOT* EXIST; AND *THUS* THEY ARE *ALL* THAT *MATTERS.* DO YOU UNDERSTAND?

136

NO.

YOU ARE *HONEST.* I'LL SAY *THAT* FOR YOU.

THERE ARE *DOORS,* TIMOTHY HUNTER. OVER THERE.

HERE IS THE *KEY*--USE IT HOW YOU WILL. A GIFT FROM ME TO YOU.

HERE-- *CATCH!*

NO!

DID I DO SOMETHING *WRONG?*

NO.

137

HAMNET? A STRAWBERRY CORDIAL, PLEASE.

YES, YOUR MAJESTY.

WELL, *GO ON,* CHILD. *YOU TOO,* ROSE. SHOW HIM THE WORLDS BEYOND REASON.

"I DID SOMETHING WRONG, DIDN'T I?"

"LATER, TIMOTHY.

"FOR NOW...

"THIS IS SKARTARIS. A WORLD WITHIN THE WORLD--HERE DINOSAURS WALK AND TIME DEFORMS AND TWISTS UPON ITSELF.

"THIS WORLD IS COMPARATIVELY EASY TO ENTER FROM YOURS.

"INDEED, AT PRESENT IT IS RULED BY A MAN FROM EARTH. BUT AS ONE TOUCHES A NEW WORLD ONE IS ALSO TOUCHED: HE IS NOW THE WORLD'S WARLORD, AS HIS DAUGHTER HAS BECOME ITS ENCHANTRESS.

"THERE.

"ANOTHER DOOR."

"THE WORLDS BEYOND CAN BE *REFUGES*, TIMOTHY. PERHAPS *EACH* OF US CREATES HIS OWN FANTASY WORLD--A PLACE TO WHICH WE CAN RETREAT. *HERE* A COUNTRY CALLED *MYRRA*, *THERE* THE LAND OF *PYTHARIA*, AND AT THE *EDGE* OF EVERY MAP, 'HERE BE DRAGONS.'

"IN YOUR WORLD *JIM ROOK* SANG SONGS OF ENLIGHTENMENT AND LOVE--UNTIL HE WAS SEIZED BY A KINGDOM OF *BLOOD* AND *ENCHANTMENT*...

"...WHERE *COMPANIONS* TO *HEROES* ARE FOREVER BRAVE AND TRUE...

"...WHERE *EVIL WIZARDS* FOREVER BROOD ON DUSTY PARCHMENT SPELLS TO RAISE THEIR ARMIES OF THE DEAD, AND THEN FOREVER FLEE, THEIR SCHEMES IN RUINS...

"... WHERE *GIANTS* FEEFIFOFUM UNTIL THEIR *HEADS* ARE *SEVERED* BY HEROES' SWORDS -- EACH BLADE *NAMED* AND *MAGICAL*.

"IN *THIS* PLACE MEN HAVE *SOBRIQUETS* LIKE *CLAW THE UNCONQUERED*, OR *STALKER THE SOULLESS*; ROOK BECAME *NIGHTMASTER*, AND WILL FIGHT TO *SAVE* THE WORLD, *OR* TO *DESTROY* IT.

"IN WORLDS SUCH AS THIS THE TERMS BECOME *SYNONYMOUS*, I AM AFRAID.

"*I*, TOO, HAVE AN ENCHANTED SWORD, THOUGH I USE IT BUT RARELY.

"ANOTHER DOOR."

"THEY CALL *THIS* PLACE *THE GEMWORLD.*

"IN YEARS PAST, *MANY* THINGS MAGICAL *FLED* YOUR WORLD: AND THEY CAME *HERE.*

"*BENEATH* THIS WORLD THE *ARCHMAGE* IS CHAINED; IT IS *HE* THAT EMPOWERS THIS WORLD, *HE* WHO MAKES IT WHAT IT IS; ALTHOUGH THOSE WHO LIVE ON THE WORLD ABOVE WOULD NOT DREAM IT.

"HERE *TWELVE* GREAT HOUSES, EACH NAMED AFTER A GEMSTONE COMMON TO THAT AREA, *PLOT* AND *COUNTERPLOT,* LIAISE, *BETRAY, MARRY* AND *MURDER.*

"HERE THE *SUN* RISES FROM THE *EASTERN SEA,* AND HAS BECOME A *MOON* BY THE TIME IT SETS IN THE *WATERS* OF THE *WEST:* AND THE *WATERS* SPILL *FOREVER* INTO THE *NIGHT.*

"ANOTHER DOOR."

"HMM. *FAERIE* AND *THIS PLACE* HAVE ALWAYS BEEN *LINKED*-- BY RIGHT OF *TITHE* IF BY NOTHING ELSE.

"THIS IS *HELL*, TIM. ONE *TINY* ASPECT OF IT, ANYWAY.

"HERE DO MANY *DEMONS* MAKE THEIR HOMES, THE TWISTED GEOMETRIES CONFORMING WITH THEIR OWN DARK INTERNAL VISTAS. THEY CAN BE *CALLED* TO OUR WORLD, FOR A *PRICE*...

" THE PRICE IS *TOO MUCH*.

" THIS IS A PLACE OF *PUNISHMENT*, TIMOTHY. THOSE WHO BELIEVE THEY MUST *ATONE*, INFLICT *THIS PLACE* AND ITS TORTURES UPON *THEMSELVES*...

"UNTIL THEY *UNDERSTAND THAT*. UNTIL THEY REALIZE THAT *THEY*, AND *ONLY THEY*-- NOT *GODS* OR *DEMONS*--*CREATE* THEIR HELL; AND BY THIS THEY ARE *FREED*, AND TAKE THEIR *LEAVE*...

" THIS PLACE IS *EVIL*, TIMOTHY. BUT PERHAPS A *NECESSARY* EVIL.

"ANOTHER DOOR."

HU-HU-HU-HU-*HURRAH!* IT, UH, IT'S MM, TIMOTHY HU-*HUNTER*!

meep.

QUIET, BOOBY. HE KNOWS WHO HE *IS*. HELLO, TIMOTHY, HELLO DOCTOR. MYSELF AND MY *FAT-HEADED* (AND *GUTTED*), NOT TO MENTION MORE-OR-LESS *BRAIN-DEAD* BROTHER WOULD LIKE TO *WELCOME* YOU TO THIS *REALM*.

HEHEHHEH. *DEAR* CHILD.

WHERE ARE WE?

THE *DREAMING*.

A REALM COMPRISING *TALES* AND *NIGHTMARES*, WOVEN ON THE FRAGILE *LOOM* OF *SLEEPING MINDS*.

AND *WE* ARE ITS *GUARDIANS* AND *PROTECTORS*, ITS *HEROES* AND ITS *LORDS*. MY BROTHER AND I-- *LORD CAIN* AND *LORD ABEL*.

REMEMBER *US*, WHEN YOU COME INTO YOUR *FULL POWER*, TIMOTHY.

"Lord" Cain? "Lord" Abel?

Tell me -- when did this elevation in rank occur? Are my congratulations in order, Tale-keepers?

AMUH-MUH-UM-BA-BAH-UWUHWUH-AHWUUH...

murp.

SHUT UP, NITWIT.

YOU are Timothy Hunter?

UM. HELLO.

THIS PLACE SEEMS SO FAMILIAR...

JUST OUR LITTLE, HEH-HEH, JEST, WITH YOUNG TIMOTHY HERE, SIRE...

Ah. I understand. Then you are welcome to this dreamworld, child, whether waking or asleep.

I am the lord of this realm, child. I am Dream.

AH.

MY LORD SHAPER WOULD BE **WELCOME** HERE. AND **YES**, TITANIA IS A NAME I **HAVE** BEEN CALLED.

MY LADY...

AH. **DOCTOR**. I WAS **WONDERING** WHEN YOU WOULD MAKE YOUR APPEARANCE. **YES?**

IT IS TIME FOR US TO **LEAVE**, MAJESTY. TIM HAS FAR TO GO BEFORE HIS JOURNEY'S END. WE **THANK YOU** FOR YOUR **HOSPITALITY**, BUT **MUST** RETURN TO OUR **OWN** WORLD.

REALLY? DOCTOR...

DID YOU TELL TIMOTHY **NOTHING** OF THE RULES OF THIS PLACE?

I TOLD HIM...

BUT, LOOK, HE TOOK A **GIFT**, IN **FAERIE**.

TIMOTHY, BOY, WILL YOU **STAY** WITH ME? WILL YOU BE MY PAGE AND SERVANT, **HERE** IN THE LANDS OF SUMMER'S TWILIGHT, WHERE THERE IS **NO AGE OR DEATH**?

YOU HAVE NOT SEEN A **FRACTION** OF THE MARVELS OF THIS WORLD, TIM. YOU HAVE NOT **TASTED** OUR **FRUIT**, NOR **DRUNK** OUR **WINE**, NOR **DANCED** TO YOUR SOUL'S DELIGHT IN OUR **REVELRIES**.

STAY. BE MY PAGE.

AND IN RETURN **I** WILL BE **ALL** THINGS TO YOU.

THANK YOU FOR THE OFFER, YOUR MAJESTY. BUT I WANT TO GO *HOME*. I DON'T *WANT* TO STAY HERE FOREVER.

I AM NOT OFFERING A *CHOICE*, TIMOTHY.

YOU.

YOU TOOK A *GIFT* FROM ME--A *SILVER KEY*. A KEY THAT UNLOCKS *WORLDS*.

YOU IN YOUR TURN NOW *OWE* A GIFT TO *ME*, TIMOTHY, A GIFT OF *EQUAL* VALUE AND WORTH.

OTHERWISE, I WILL BE *FORCED* TO TAKE...

I HAVE TO GO *HOME*. MY DAD *NEEDS* ME. I MEAN, I'M NOTHING *SPECIAL*. I WANT TO GO HOME.

IT'S *TOO LATE*. STAY HERE *WILLINGLY*, OR STAY HERE *AGAINST* YOUR *WILL*.

OR DOWER ME A *GIFT*--AS VALUABLE AS THE *KEY* TO *WORLDS*.

I APOLOGIZE FOR THIS, TIMOTHY. I *WISH* YOU HAD HEEDED MY WARNING; BUT DO NOT *DESPAIR*.

MYSELF AND THE OTHER THREE WILL *RETURN*. WE WILL FREE YOU *SOME-HOW*, THOUGH WE MUST *RAZE* HALF OF FAERIE TO SO DO.

IT IS--YOU ARE-- OUR *RESPONSIBILITY*, AFTER ALL.

WHAT? YOU MEAN, YOU AREN'T GOING TO *STOP* HER?

NO.

RULES ARE *RULES*, HERE AS MUCH AS *ANYWHERE ELSE*.

AN *EYE* FOR AN *ISLAND*, A *TOOTH* FOR A *TOOTH* FAIRY.

RULES ARE *RULES*.

NO! I'M NOT *STAYING HERE*! THIS IS *RIDICULOUS*!

VERY WELL. THEN *WHAT* WILL YOU OFFER ME IN EXCHANGE FOR MY FINE KEY?

I DON'T *HAVE* ANYTHING SPECIAL.

EVEN THE THING I GOT AT THE *MARKET* WAS JUST *NORMAL*. THAT *GLORY* BLOKE SAID SO.

WHAT DID YOU GET AT THE MARKET, TIM?

AN *ORDINARY EGG*, HE CALLED IT, DOCTOR. MADE OF *AMBER*, OR SOMETHING.

THE MUNDANE EGG.

THAT'S WHAT I *MEANT*. NORMAL. BORING. MUNDANE. I *KNEW* IT WAS ONE OF *THOSE* WORDS.

NO, TIMOTHY. IT *ISN'T* ONE OF *THOSE* WORDS AT ALL. NOT IN *THIS* CONTEXT.

WHY? WHAT'S SO *SPECIAL* ABOUT IT?

INSIDE THIS EGG IS A PART OF CREATION AS YET *UNBORN*. ONE DAY THE EGG WILL *HATCH*-- AND FROM IT A *WORLD* WILL EMERGE.

EVERY WORLD IS *HATCHED* FROM A *MUNDANE EGG*, TIMOTHY.

AND THEY *ARE* VALUABLE.

YOUR MAJESTY: WILL YOU DO US THE *HONOR* OF ACCEPTING TIMOTHY'S GIFT?

I HAVE NO *CHOICE*. RULES ARE *RULES*.

STRANGE. I HAD THOUGHT THE LAST MUNDANE EGG HATCHED *LONG* SINCE.

VERY WELL.

YOU MAY *GO--BOTH* OF YOU.

GO....

...BEFORE I CHANGE MY MIND.

AND WILL *YOU ALSO* HATCH OUT *WORLDS,* MY SON?

149

TIM? WAKE UP.

WE'RE BACK.

THAT'S RIGHT.

WE AREN'T *ANYWHERE FUNNY,* ARE WE?

NO. IT'S OVER.

WHAT DO I DO WITH *THIS?*

IT'S *YOURS.* IT WAS A FAIR TRADE, AFTER ALL. *KEEP IT.* PERHAPS *ONE* DAY YOU'LL FIND THE *DOOR* THAT *KEY* WILL *FIT.*

WELL, THAT'S *ENDED.*

THIS PART OF YOUR TRAVELS, YES.

ONLY *ONE* MORE JOURNEY TO GO, THEN; ONLY ONE MORE GUIDE: THE BLIND GUY. MISTER E.

SO. WHERE *NOW?*

TOMORROW.

THAT'S *WHEN* WE LEAVE?

NO, TIMOTHY.

THAT'S *WHERE* YOU'RE GOING...

I HEARD A *JOKE* ABOUT YOU, ONCE, E.

A JOKE?

I THINK IT WAS A JOKE. BLOKE I MET IN A BAR IN KHATMANDU. SAID YOU *ALWAYS* CARRIED A POCKET FULL OF STAKES, IN CASE YOU MET A *VAMPIRE;* AND A GUN LOADED WITH *SILVER BULLETS,* IN CASE YOU EVER MET A *WEREWOLF.*

BLIMEY.

I TAKE IT YOU HAMMER FIRST AND ASK QUESTIONS AFTERWARDS.

THE ONLY *GOOD* VAMPIRE IS A *DEAD* VAMPIRE, CONSTANTINE.

I'M SURE THEY'D AGREE WITH YOU ON THAT SCORE.

YOU OUGHT TO *WATCH* IT, YOU KNOW. ONE DAY THE BOGEYMEN ARE GOING TO COME OUT OF THEIR CLOSETS AND START PARADING DOWN THE HIGH STREET.

THEY'LL BE MARCHING FOR *EQUAL* RIGHTS, *FREE* BLOOD, AND *YOUR* HEAD ON A PLATTER.

IS THAT SOME KIND OF *JOKE,* CONSTANTINE?

IF YOU'RE *LUCKY.*

CIGARETTE?

UNLIKE YOU, I DO NOT DEFILE THE TEMPLE OF MY BODY, CONSTANTINE.

IN *THAT* CASE, I SUPPOSE A QUICK--

QUIET, YOU TWO. THEY ARE RETURNING.

153

THEY'VE BEEN GONE A WHILE. WHAT EXACTLY IS E MEANT TO BE *SHOWING* THE KID?

THE RISE AND FALL OF MAGIC, IN THE YEARS TO COME. A THOUSAND YEARS INTO THE FUTURE, PERHAPS. NO MORE.

LATER THAN THAT, AND IT BECOMES INCREASINGLY DIFFICULT TO RETURN TO THE HERE AND NOW.

I WOULD NOT *QUESTION* YOUR JUDGMENT, SIR. BUT *WHY* DID YOU CHOOSE E?

I HAVE HEARD *DISTURBING* THINGS ABOUT HIM, IN THE PAST.

PERHAPS. BUT ONE MUST USE THE VESSELS AVAILABLE.

REMEMBER, HE FOUGHT VALIANTLY IN CALCUTTA. HE HAS ALWAYS SOUGHT TO UPHOLD GOODNESS AND LIGHT, AS HE HAS PERCEIVED IT. HE IS ABLE--AS WE ARE NOT --TO SHOW THE CHILD THE TIMES YET TO COME.

AND THERE IS ANOTHER REASON.

WHICH IS?

BALANCE, JOHN CONSTANTINE.

13

MAGIC

FREE WILL. THERE MUST ALWAYS BE FREE WILL.

BOLLOCKS.

SHOULDN'T THEY BE *BACK* BY NOW?

YES.

IS THERE A *PROBLEM?*

I AM AFRAID SO, JOHN CONSTANTINE.

THEY ARE LOST TO ME. WHEREVER THEY HAVE GONE, IT IS SO FAR IN THE FUTURE THAT I CAN NO LONGER FEEL THEM. OCCULT?

YES. THEY ARE GONE, COMPLETELY.

THIS IS *RIDICULOUS!* WHAT ARE YOU *SAYING?* THAT THEY'VE HEADED OFF INTO THE *FAR FUTURE,* AND THERE'S *NOTHING* YOU CAN DO TO GET THEM *BACK?*

YES.

I CAN'T *BELIEVE* IT--YOU'D TRUST *TIM* TO A *LOONY* WHOSE *DAD* POPPED OUT HIS *EYES* WITH A *SHARPENED SPOON?* I MEAN, AFTER WHAT HAPPENED TO *HIM* AND HIS *SISTER,* IT'S HARDLY *SURPRISING* THAT HE'S NOT DEALING WITH A *FULL DECK,* IS IT?

I CAN'T BELIEVE YOU *DID* IT.

THERE ARE BEDS OF *KELP* SMARTER THAN YOU, MATE!

I HAVE MADE A MISTAKE, CONSTANTINE. I REALIZE THAT.

I APOLOGIZE.

THAT'S NOT GOING TO BRING TIM BACK. HE'S JUST A *KID.* HE TRUSTED US TO KEEP HIM SAFE. I *DON'T...*

--BELIEVE IT. WE KNOW. TO *ERR* IS HUMAN, JOHN CONSTANTINE.

IF *HE'S* HUMAN, THEN *I'M* A TOAST-RACK.

WE MUST CONCENTRATE OUR EFFORTS ON GETTING THEM BACK. THIS BICKERING IS FUTILE.

CAN'T YOU *REACH* THEM? AREN'T THERE ANY *GODS* OR *DEMONS* OR *ANYTHING* YOU COULD SEND TO GET THEM *BACK?*

NO.

BUT YOU HAVE HIT ON SOMETHING...

DOCTOR OCCULT. THE RAPTOR IS TIM'S...

LISTEN, NIGHT-BIRD. TIMOTHY, YOUR MASTER: WHEREVER HE IS--WHEREVER HE MIGHT BE. *FIND* HIM. *PROTECT* HIM. *HELP* HIM. MY *FRIEND*-- LEND ME *STRENGTH. CONSTANTINE--* LEND ME *WILL.* LEND ME *FAITH.*

GO.

I NOTICE YOU DIDN'T TELL THE BIRD TO BRING HIM BACK.

IF HE HAS GONE THAT FAR IN THE FUTURE, CONSTANTINE, IT IS UNLIKELY THAT THERE IS ANY FORCE THAT CAN BRING HIM BACK TO US.

SO *NOW* WHAT?

WE WAIT.

I WISH YOU'D STOP *SAYING* THAT.

175

SO THIS IS IT, THEN?

IT WOULD SEEM SO.

YES.

THE CHARGE OF THE TRENCHCOAT BRIGADE.

"THEIRS NOT TO MAKE REPLY, THEIRS BUT TO DO AND DIE, INTO THE VALLEY OF DEATH RODE THE SIX HUNDRED."

TENNYSON NEVER STRUCK ME AS YOUR KIND OF POET, JOHN CONSTANTINE.

LEARNED IT IN DETENTION AT SCHOOL, DIDN'T I? I COULDN'T HAVE BEEN MUCH OLDER THAN TIM AT THE TIME.

YOU KNOW, WE REALLY MESSED THIS ONE UP.

NOT ENTIRELY. WE CLOSED DOWN THE BROTHERHOOD OF THE COLD FLAME, AFTER ALL. AND THEY WOULD HAVE KILLED TIMOTHY.

SO INSTEAD WE HANDED HIM OVER TO A MANIAC WHO'S DONE THE JOB FOR THEM. TERRIFIC.

ONE DAY ANOTHER CHILD WILL COME. AND WHEN THAT DAY COMES, WE WILL HAVE LEARNED FROM THIS--

YOU ARE OUT OF YOUR TINY MIND, IF YOU THINK I'M EVER GOING TO GET INVOLVED IN ANOTHER OF YOUR BLOODY FIASCOS--

STOP IT! BOTH OF YOU!

YEAH. STOP IT. I'M NOT DEAD OR ANYTHING. I'M FINE, I THINK.

TIM!

WELCOME, CHILD.

WE ARE PLEASED TO SEE YOU.

THERE WAS THIS WOMAN THERE. AT THE END OF TIME. SHE SENT ME BACK HERE.

AND E?

SHE SAID HE'D HAVE TO FIND HIS OWN WAY BACK. SHE SAID HE WAS GOING TO HAVE TO WALK.

IT WILL BE A LONG WALK, FROM ETERNITY TO HERE. HE HAS MY SYMPATHIES.

EVEN AFTER HE TRIED TO KILL TIM?

I AM AFRAID SO.

WHERE IS YOUR *OWL*, TIMOTHY?

HE SAVED MY *LIFE*. E WAS GOING TO *KILL* ME...

IT WAS A *GOOD* SOUL. IT *CARED* FOR YOU.

YEAH. *RIGHT*. THANKS. CAN'T YOU BRING HIM BACK?

13

NO.

SO I'M BACK. I'VE BEEN ALL THE WAY TO THE END OF TIME, AND I'M *BACK*.

JOHN-- *YOU* WERE THERE.

WHAT?

NOTHING.

SO, TIMOTHY. YOU HAVE SEEN WHAT WE HAVE SHOWN YOU. YOU HAVE SEEN THE PAST. YOU HAVE MET A HANDFUL OF THE PRESENT PRACTITIONERS OF THE ART.

YOU HAVE GLIMPSED THE WORLDS THAT TOUCH YOUR OWN.

YOU HAVE SEEN THE BEGINNING, AND YOU HAVE SEEN THE END.

NOW, YOURS IS THE DECISION.

IF YOU CHOOSE MAGIC, YOU WILL NEVER BE ABLE TO RETURN TO THE LIFE YOU ONCE LIVED. YOUR WORLD MAY BE MORE...EXCITING... BUT IT WILL ALSO BE MORE DANGEROUS. LESS RELIABLE.

AND ONCE YOU BEGIN TO WALK THE PATH OF MAGIC, YOU CAN NEVER STEP OFF IT.

OR YOU CAN CHOOSE THE PATH OF SCIENCE, OF RATIONALITY. LIVE IN A NORMAL WORLD. DIE A NORMAL DEATH. LESS EXCITING, UNDOUBTEDLY. BUT SAFER.

THE *CHOICE* IS *YOURS.*

UM....

I'M *SORRY.*

I...

I APPRECIATE WHAT YOU'VE DONE FOR ME. ALL THE STUFF I'VE *SEEN.* ALL THAT.

BUT I'VE LEARNED A *LOT* OF THINGS. THE MAIN THING I'VE LEARNED IS THAT IT ALL HAS A *PRICE.* I MEAN, YOU CAN GET WHATEVER YOU WANT. BUT IT ALL HAS TO BE *PAID* FOR, *DOESN'T* IT?

AND I DON'T *WANT* TO PAY WHAT IT'LL *COST.* I'M *SCARED.*

I'M *SORRY.*

ARE YOU *ANGRY?*

193

... I SAID I DIDN'T WANT ANYTHING TO DO WITH IT. I SHOULD HAVE STUCK TO MY GUNS.

FINAL SCORE? TIM LOSES HIS ONE AND ONLY CHANCE AT MAGIC, WE LOSE MISTER E--WHO'S MAKING HIS OWN WAY BACK FROM THE END OF TIME--AND...

WELL?

IT'S ALL BEEN A BIT OF A WASHOUT, HASN'T IT?

IT'S STRANGE, CONSTANTINE. ALL THE THINGS I HAVE HEARD ABOUT YOU... NO ONE EVER TOLD ME THAT YOU WERE STUPID.

WHAT? NOW LISTEN--

NO. YOU LISTEN. LISTEN AND THINK.

WE TOLD TIMOTHY THAT WE WOULD GIVE HIM A CHOICE, DID WE NOT? AND WE DID. AND THEN OUR FRIEND SHOWED HIM TIMES GONE, INTRODUCING HIM TO THE PRINCIPLES OF MAGIC.

AND YOU SHOWED HIM THAT THE WORLD WAS, INDEED, NOT THE RATIONAL PLACE HE BELIEVED.

I HAVE SHOWN HIM THE WORLD THAT IS NOT THIS WORLD, WHERE IT IS ALWAYS SUMMER'S TWILIGHT; AND OTHER PLACES BESIDES.

E GAVE HIM A FEW CHOICE FRAGMENTS OF POSSIBILITY; AND THEN TIM RETURNED TO THE FIELDS WE KNOW.

HE HAS SEEN MAGIC. HE KNOWS IT WORKS. HE HAS ALREADY WALKED A HARDER PATH THAN MOST INITIATES WILL EVER DREAM OF...

YOU.... *LIED* TO HIM.

I DID *NOT* LIE TO HIM, CONSTANTINE. I TOLD HIM THE CHOICE WAS HIS, AND INDEED, IT WAS.

AND *HE* MADE *HIS* CHOICE, WHEN FIRST WE MET.

I'LL COME WITH YOU. WHERE ARE WE *GOING?*

AND PEOPLE ACCUSE *ME* OF BEING MANIPULATIVE.

NOW WHAT?

FOR NOW, JOHN CONSTANTINE, I THINK WE OUGHT TO *WAIT.* OBSERVE THE BOY.

THEY SAY HUMANITY ONLY GETS ONE CHANCE AT THE CAROUSEL'S GOLDEN RING.

BUT THE CAROUSEL GOES ROUND AND ROUND, AND ROUND AND ROUND. AND THE GOLDEN RING IS NOT GOING ANYWHERE.

YOU'RE QUITE THE LITTLE *ROMANTIC,* AREN'T YOU? *NAH,* DON'T *ANSWER* THAT. RUIN YOUR *IMAGE.* SO WE JUST WAIT AND SEE?

WE WILL WAIT.

AND WE WILL *SEE.*

195

TIM?

UH.

I DON'T *NEED* YOU LOT. I DON'T NEED *ANYTHING.*

ALL I NEED TO DO IS *BELIEVE.*

MAGIC!

DEDICATION

To Diana Wynne Jones, Jane Yolen, Ellen Kushner and Terri Windling: four witches.

ACKNOWLEDGMENTS

In my school holidays, when I was much younger, I would spend whole days at our local library, reading my way through the children's section. It was a magical journey, or rather, a succession of journeys, in a small room full of books.

Writing this tale I found myself greatly indebted to that nine-year-old me, sitting somewhere with a book; and to the people who took me to wonderlands.

I owe a huge debt to all those arcane practitioners and master magicians: Edith Nesbitt and P.L. Travers and Edward Eager, C.S. Lewis and Andrew Lang, Margaret Storey and Noel Langley, Lewis Carroll and J.P. Martin, Nicholas Stuart Gray and J.B.S. Haldane and Clive King and T.H. White — and the rest: there are many others, many of whose names I have by now forgotten or never knew. They were the first to tell me that there was magic, and where it was to be found.

Rachel Pollack gave me Tarot advice, Marv Wolfman explained Baron Winter, and Bob Greenberger kibitzed on continuity. The late Arthur Waley's translations of oriental poems helped to assemble the tale of the Wu woman, and Karen Berger, editor extraordinary, forgave me for sneakily writing a novel when I should have been working on this.

So to them, and to John Bolton, Scott Hampton, Charles Vess, and Paul Johnson, and also to Mike Dringenberg, Tom Yeates, Paul Chadwick, John Ridgway, Ron Randall, Todd Klein, and the mysterious Mister Zed: my thanks.

— Neil Gaiman

A P O C R Y P H A

Preliminary incantations for THE BOOKS OF MAGIC
from Neil Gaiman, Charles Vess and Paul Johnson

Pencilled art by Charles Vess for Book Three.

Magic Book 3

Hi Charles.

Well, we knocked them dead with Shakespeare. Now let's see what we can do with Magic...

Basically, the way I see this issue, is as a journey to fairyland comic. Were we totally true to our sources, Tim wouldn't get out for seven years, or seventy, at the end; and he'd also be in far more danger than we're going to put him in.

However he's under the guardianship of Dr Occult (and of Rose Psychic, Occult's _anima_. He's under the protection of Yo-yo the owl, who ought to be able to talk in fairyland. And he's a bright enough kid to know that he oughtn't to do the things he's told not to do.

Having said that, I may have him do something he oughtn't, like accept a gift, or ask a question, to give him something to get out of, or even to have someone else sacrifice themselves for him.

I've noted down a list of ingredients, anyway, that I'll try and include. In some ways it's a real pity that I had to do this one last, because it means I can't do anything drastic to anyone, but let's just see what happens.

***

It's sunset: Dr Occult and Tim are walking down an English country lane toward us. Tim is dressed as he was at the end of issue 2, although he's also wearing any coat or jacket he might have picked up during issue 2. The sun is setting, and though they aren't actually walking by the old man of Wilmington, we're into that territory. Like the Ashdown forest area we wandered through when you were over here, Charles. It's late autumn.

Are you a real doctor?

Am I a real doctor of what?

I don't know.

I'm not a medical doctor, if that's what you mean, child, although I can set a bone or stench the flow of blood if need be.

Dr Occult. It's a funny name.

Name?

Thing to be called, then. What are we waiting for?

'The sun to set. We must leave in Twilight.

They stop here. Tim reaches up to an apple tree above them, and pulls down a late apple from the tree, small and yellowing, and commences to munch it, cheerfully.

Will you tell me something?

Possibly.

You four. Who are you? I mean, Constantine, he's just a bloke, isn't he?

John Constantine...

Yes. He dances on the edge of the known, like a crazy man, pitting himself against heaven and the pit, because he is John Constantine; and because he is ~~human, and is~~ alive.

How about E? Is he really blind?

Oh yes. He... He is an extremist. He fights what he ~~perceives~~ reas the forces of darkness; but sometimes I suspect that all he ever sees is darkness... But he can ~~see~~, ways that I cannot. travel even

And the other one? He spooks me...

The stranger? Ahh. I have encountered him, in the past. He also walks his own path. One that began too long ago, and I suspect, ~~for him there is~~ has no end in sight.

I do not know his story. I know none who does; although I have heard conjectures aplenty: that he is the wandering Jew, or the angel who neither fell with lucifer nor fight with Michael, or...

But There are ~~other~~ guesses. Some say he owes alliegance to order, or to chaos, or to man: speculations all. I do not know what he is. And perhaps he has walked to forget ~~enough~~ that he ~~does not know~~ himself. no loger remember. so long ~~remember~~

Ah. And you, a occult?

I am your guide through this stage of your journey, Timothy Hunter. And you may trust me.

Empty your pockets.

Leave the keys and the coins here -- tie them in your kerchief, perhaps. Cold iron will not be welcome where we go. The rest you may retain. They will be the same as before.

Listen to me carefully, now. There are things you must remember.

Firstly, on our journey, you must obey my orders explicitly and in all things, no matter how petty or strange they seem to you.

Secondly, ask no questions or favours of those you meet on our travels; and accept no gifts, or foodstuffs, or favours, save with my blessing.

Thirdly, remember your manners: etiquette will be important where we go, and good manners are gold. For impoliteness you could find yourself gifted with asses' ears, or worse. a trivial

Lastly, never stray from the path. No matter what you see, or hear, or feel.

Do you understand?

I suppose so.

Good.

Then we are ready to begin our journey.

Um. Doctor Occult?

Yes.

Constantine said we were going to Fairyland. He was kidding, wasn't he?

We are going to the fair lands, child. Call them Avalon, or Everywhere, or Dom-Daniel, or Fairyland, it matters not. We are going to the Land of Summer's Twilight.

Oh.

Wait here. I will walk across to that wicket gate. When I wave to you, then walk as I walked, along that path. When you cross the stream, before the gate, take care not to get your feet wet. Yes?

Fine.

(Occult walks off.)

Yo-yo? Why are we doing this? I mean, why am I doing this stuff? Anyone with half an ounce of sense would have told them to bugger off at the beginning...

Oh well. Too late now.

Here goes.

(He walks down the hill. Occult has his back to us, raincoat and hat. I'd suggest doing this in long, vertical panels. tim walks

•down the hill in a long pull back, toward this tiny figure of DR Occult, just walking casually on an autumn evening

He crosses the stream.
Occult ~~keeps~~ keeps his back to us.
Tim: So I'm here. How do we go to fairyland.
Doc Occult turns: he's now a woman, wearing occult's coat and hat, but a red dress beneath it.
Doc: Look behind you, child.
He turns: Looking against the shore is the sea, here the stream was.
Tim: But...
Occult: that wicket gate is in both territories. Here and also There.
And it is inside your mind. Because you are English we came here from England and we got here. From other places we would have come to the dreamtime or the dusty gound, or to the world forest, or to many another place: and they would all be here. Realities are unstable.
~~were~~ does the path go now?
"Through the gate."

"That is right. Now, once through the wicket gate you may notice how things will change."

"Like what?"

"You will notice how you see them. Come."
go through the gate & over the page. And we're in the land of summer's twilight - the path travels 3 ways: 2 go off the page centre, glowing path leads to a beautiful gold city. It's lovely.
Now we get Rose Psychic. He exclaims & amazement ~~asks~~ is the occult who says no, although they share much including memory. she begins to ask her new who her name is then corrects himself.

Thumbnail layouts and finished pencils
by Charles Vess for Book Three.

HERE
LIES
BABY
21 DEC. 1855 · 3 JAN 1886

Thumbnail layouts by Paul Johnson for Book Four.

NEIL GAIMAN lives mostly in America with two cats, two large white dogs and a number of awards from all over the world. He still does not understand how he came to be responsible for the feeding and domestic arrangements of these animals, nor, for that matter, what he is doing living in America. He has seven beehives and many bees. He has written novels and comics and movies and TV and poems and an opera and he keeps a Twitter feed, which is nothing like keeping bees at all. He is married to punk cabaret chanteuse Amanda Palmer and has played himself in animated televisual cartoons.

JOHN BOLTON began his art career in the late 1970s, illustrating stories for such British magazines as *Look In*, *The House of Hammer* and *Hammer's Halls of Horror*. After breaking into the American comics market with a story in Marvel Comics' *Bizarre Adventures*, Bolton became a regular contributor to Marvel's anthology title *Epic Illustrated* and the Epic comics imprint, where both his pen-and-ink and painted art styles were showcased in the series *Kull the Conqueror* and *The Black Dragon* and the graphic novels *Marada the She-Wolf* and *Someplace Strange*. Bolton began his association with DC Comics and Vertigo in 1990 with his work on Neil Gaiman's THE BOOKS OF MAGIC, and has since illustrated a host of titles for them, including BATMAN: THE MAN-BAT, BATMAN/JOKER: SWITCH, MENZ INSANA, USER, GIFTS OF THE NIGHT, THE SANDMAN PRESENTS: THE FURIES and GOD SAVE THE QUEEN. He spends most of his time painting in a studio lined with eerie movie props and esoteric books.

SCOTT HAMPTON began his comics career following in the footsteps of his brother and fellow comic book creator Bo Hampton. Both Scott and Bo studied under Will Eisner in 1976, and in 1981 Scott's first professional work — the three-page story "Victims" — appeared in Warren Publishing's *Vampirella* #101. Hampton has gone on to illustrate such iconic properties as Batman, Lucifer, Black Widow, Hellraiser, and Star Trek, as well as crafting such creator-owned titles as *The Upturned Stone* (Kitchen Sink Press) and *Spookhouse* (IDW Publishing) in which he adapted his favorite ghost stories into sequential form. From 2007 to 2009 he collaborated with writer Steve Niles on an 18-issue run of SIMON DARK for DC Comics, and he is currently working on another Neil Gaiman multi-artist project: a two-volume graphic novel adaptation of *The Graveyard Book* for HarperCollins.

The award-winning work of **CHARLES VESS** has graced both covers and pages for numerous comics and mainstream publishers, including DC, Marvel, Dark Horse, Viking, Tor and HarperCollins. His work has been featured in numerous gallery and museum exhibitions in the U.S. and abroad, and his awards include an Ink Pot, two World Fantasies, the Mythopoeic, a Gold and Silver Spectrum Annual, two Chesleys, a Locus for Best Artist and two Will Eisner Comic Industry Awards. He also shared the prestigious World Fantasy Award for Best Short Story with Neil Gaiman in 1991 for their collaboration on THE SANDMAN #19, "A Midsummer Night's Dream." The two reunited to produce the illustrated fantasy novel NEIL GAIMAN AND CHARLES VESS' STARDUST, which was adapted in 2007 into an acclaimed motion picture.

Rising up from the self-publishing and small press peripheries of the early 1980s British comics scene, **PAUL JOHNSON** hit the big time in 1989 with the James Robinson-written graphic novel *London's Dark*. His subsequent work on Neil Gaiman's acclaimed miniseries THE BOOKS OF MAGIC led to a variety of assignments from DC (MERCY, THE INVISIBLES), Marvel (*Interface*, *Children of the Voyager*), and Dark Horse (*Aliens: Sacrifice*), and eventually took him back to England as a contributor to the anthology titles *Crisis*, *2000 AD* and *Spinechillers*. After 15 years in the industry, however, Johnson decided to pursue a different calling, and he spent much of the following decade studying acupuncture and traditional Chinese medicine in the UK and China. He now splits his time between lecturing on traditional Chinese medicine in London and treating patients in his private clinic in Surrey.

One of the industry's most versatile and accomplished letterers, **TODD KLEIN** has been lettering comics since 1977 and has won numerous Eisner and Harvey Awards for his work. A highlight of his career has been working with Neil Gaiman on nearly all the original issues of THE SANDMAN, as well as BLACK ORCHID, DEATH: THE HIGH COST OF LIVING, DEATH: THE TIME OF YOUR LIFE and THE BOOKS OF MAGIC.